BALLET

THE
WONDERFUL NEW
BOOK OF

BALLET

BY EDWINA HAZARD GLEN

RAND McNALLY & COMPANY
Chicago · New York · San Francisco

PICTURE CREDITS:
*American Ballet Theatre,
58, 60B; Ballet Russe de
Monte Carlo, 19, 45A, 52A, 62,
64; Basch, 88-9; Beaton
(Payne), 83B; Capezio, 18;
Constantine, 65; Danielian
(Bruce), 32A; Dribben, 52C;
Fehl, (New York City Ballet),
8, 48-9, 76, 79B, 86,
(American Ballet Theatre),
33, 36, 44, 50, 55B & C,
57, 85B; Fordyce, 43; Henle
(Monkmeyer), 42, 56, 61;
Hurok Artists, 79A; Lacey,
26-7; LaSalle, 41; Leipzig, 14,
20A & B, 21, 22-3, 28B, 38-9;
McCracken, 84A;
New York City Ballet,
12A, 45B-E, 59, 85A;
New York Public Library
(Dance Archives), 60, 66-74,
80A; New York Times, 24-5;
Oleaga, cover, 59B, 82-3, 84B;
Seymour (NYCB), 9, (ABT),
6, 83, 84C; (BR de MC), 63;
Swope, 34, 40A & B;
52B, 53A-C; Wood, 54.*

*The Publishers are grateful to
Selma Jeanne Cohen,
of the Dance Archives of the New York
Public Library, for her help
in checking the accuracy of this book.*

1-BALLET
page 6

**4-THE BALLET
COMPANY**
page 50

Erik Bruhn and Lupe Serrano dance the beautiful pas de deux *from Act II of Swan Lake*

Chapter One

BALLET

*Your first ballet—and you sit
spellbound in the audience as you
watch a great performance*

A hush settles over the crowded theater. The house lights dim as the footlights go on and make the great gold curtain glow. In the pit, the orchestra begins to play.

You sit forward, your hands clasped tight in your lap. On stage, the most exciting kind of dancing in the world is about to begin. The theater is filled with the sweet song of the violins.

Slowly the curtain rises.

The stage is bathed in ghostly moonlight and you see that you are at the side of a lake. A cluster of beautiful white swans, led by a swan queen wearing a crown, glides across the lake's surface. The ballet has begun.

Then a handsome young prince and his party of hunters enter. While the prince watches in amazement, a lovely creature dances onto the scene. She is part woman, part swan. Dressed all in white, with feathers framing her face, she wears the glittering crown. Her fluttering movements of head, hands and feet are rapid and birdlike, while her bearing and grace show you that she is very feminine and regal.

The other swans—young girls who have been transformed by a magician—seem to flow on stage in a wave of sparkling white, proud sleek heads, strong slender necks, and long twinkling legs. There is a gasp of appreciation and a burst of applause from the audience for these dazzling young creatures, palely glowing in the moonlight.

After the swans' dance, the queen joins the hunter prince in a *pas de deux*, or dance for two.

The swan queen is a role in which a dancer must excel, if she is to become a fine artist.

Here she is surrounded by swan-girls. The ballerina in this picture, Melissa Hayden

How beautiful the prima ballerina is! What effortless movements carry her about the stage! You can feel the audience all around you responding to her, delighting in her superb control, the weightless marvel of her leaps, and the pride her whole body takes in performing a perfect arabesque.

You are glad you know that an arabesque is done by standing with one leg extended behind you, one arm forward and one back. You have recognized and identified this and several other movements in the ballerina's solo, and you have noticed how strong and beautiful the other swans are in their group movements. You realize that the dancers in the corps de ballet who have been singled out for the exquisite dance of the nine swan maidens must be especially good. You are glad that you now understand most all the steps they are expected to

The gracious bearing of the queen combines qualities that are both feminine and regal

no matter how satisfying a good television performance of ballet is, you get an added sense of excitement from seeing "the real thing." The expressions on the dancers' faces seem much more vivid, their smiles more dazzling, their eyes deeper and more brilliant than the screen transmitted them to you. This, you can't help but say to yourself, as you sit on the edge of your seat, is *alive*. Why, you can hear the dancers' toe shoes squeak once in a while as they dance close to the footlights.

Even if your interest in ballet is as an observer, someone who does not intend to be a professional student, your knowledge of the classroom comes alive for you now. All at once, you can understand what the lessons have meant. The shimmering figure of the ballerina, gliding, leaping and running in a series of incredible little steps, is everything you want to be yourself. When she moves, she appears to float above the ground; when she stops, she stops with such complete stillness that you catch your breath. She is like a perfect jewel, giving light from every angle, smooth and cool on the surface, showing sparks of fire deep inside.

How does the ballerina in *Swan Lake* manage to tell you that she is unhappy, using every part of her body without ever losing her poise and grace? To express her sadness, she uses the traditional gestures of pantomime. Forlornly, she indicates tears streaming down her face with her fingertips. Then she buries her face in her hands.

execute because you are a student of dance.

If you have already had some instruction, you probably started with rhythms when you were very little, and when you were about seven you began pre-ballet training. You may have had small parts in recitals at your school, and watched *The Nutcracker* on television, but this is the first live, professional ballet company you have ever seen. And

Her partner, the premier danseur, comforts and embraces her, although he, too, is sad at the thought of their parting. Together they dance a wonderful adagio that expresses their love for each other. The prince supports the swan queen in her extensions and catches her at the end of her leaps and turns. Her safety is in his strength.

What does it feel like to sail through the air and be caught in space? How does she manage to *look* like that? Not a wisp of hair is ever out of place. Every gesture is deliberate and pure. You know that if she chose she could leap higher, turn faster, and hold her extensions longer. But her role does not require such acrobatics.

For the first time you fully recognize the discipline demanded by a part and the discipline demanded of the dancer. She must always work within an established framework. Her job is to give her technique and personality to a pattern

The premier danseur must bring to his role both manly strength and grace of movement

of set movement. If she succeeds in giving this pattern her own individuality while keeping within the classic frame, then she is an artist. You settle in your seat to observe, to study, to learn, to dream.

In your classes, you have known the wonderful sensation of running to music. You have learned to leap and do turns. Now you can see how these basic steps really should look, and you realize how much work the ballerina and her partner must have done before they could achieve such perfection.

When the curtain falls at intermission, you blink as the house lights come up, and shake yourself a little to make sure where you are. You look around you at the theater, its seats filled with people of all ages, men and women and young boys and girls, who have been as thrilled as you to live for a few moments in the fairyland world of *Swan Lake*. A few seats from you in your row is a dainty little girl, younger than you, whose hands are clasped in front of her in wild excitement. She is trying to say what she has felt to a pretty woman who must be her mother. You decide to walk outside.

Out in the lobby, you try to think more about what you have just seen. This was the short version, or Act II, of *Swan Lake*. It is a touching story. The swan queen is under the spell of a wicked magician and can only become a woman between midnight and dawn. She and the prince fall deeply in love, but she is forced to leave him when the rays of morning begin to appear.

Tschaikovsky's music is hauntingly familiar. You have probably heard it several times, but now that you have seen it danced you can appreciate how well music and choreography, or dance pattern, complement each other.

Now you take a look around the theater lobby. Hanging on the walls are photographs of the members of the New York City Ballet, the company you have come to see. Some of the dancers are leaping joyously into the air, while others spin in flawless line. There is the lovely ballerina you think of as your ideal. She smiles down at you from the picture, and your mind wanders. . . .

You are in the center of a brilliantly lighted stage, smiling out over the footlights. You are wearing a white tutu (the ballet dancer's skirt that is made of layers and layers of net) and you have on satin toe slippers. Your posture is regal and proud. A rose-colored spot

In a lyrical setting, the premier danseur holds the prima ballerina in a classic arabesque

light beams down, and warm applause surrounds you. Graciously, you sweep in a deep curtsy, bowing your head demurely and spreading your arms out to the audience. An usher runs down the aisle to hand you a bouquet of red roses. . . .

You wake up with a start. The bell has rung for the second ballet and the audience is filing back inside. On the way, you pass a mirror and glance at your reflection—your pony tail (which could do with a combing), your bulky sweater (which doesn't really hide the fact that you don't stand up very straight), your scuffed flats (which definitely do not shine). How can *you* ever hope to be like that splendid creature you worshipped just a few moments ago? Angrily, you pull in your stomach and throw back your shoulders. Your chin goes in and your head sits straighter on your neck. There, that's a little better.

While you may be a long way from that girl in the spotlight, you have made a start. Your posture may be far from ideal, but you know how to correct it, if only you could remember to do so more often. Your walk already has the stamp of the dancer—your feet are planted firmly on the ground with each step and your legs swing from the hip.

You feel taller and leaner as you take your seat, and there is a new intentness in your face as you watch.

While you follow the opening steps of the second ballet, you yearn once more to be able to soar through the air like a

The swans are really young girls, changed into birds by an evil, powerful magician

gleaming bird, to make your body obey every command, to have the bearing of a queen.

This is the magical world of ballet. It cannot be entered by just anyone. Certain physical characteristics, certain artistic abilities, certain personality traits are essential to any girl or boy who wants to be a ballet dancer. These requirements will be discussed in later chapters.

If, however, you now feel that you have a sincere desire to work and learn, the patience and perseverance necessary for the years of training ahead of you, and a true love of the ballet performance, this is the time to explore the realities of the world behind the gold velvet curtains.

Let's see how you begin.

13

Your school or community group will give occasional recitals for students' families and friends

Chapter Two

HOW YOU BEGIN

Where will you study ballet?
How will you choose a teacher? What
will your schedule be?

Here you are, really at the very beginning. You're filled with visions of beautiful ballerinas, of sugar plum fairies and fiery birds. You know that you want to be one of them, to play these roles yourself. How do you begin? It's very simple. As with every other thing that is worth having, you must work to have it. As soon as you are eight years old, you are ready to go to work.

It would be wise here to consider the schedule you are embarking on and the progress you should expect to make. There are many exceptions to the following time table, but it can be used as an average guide. From the ages of eight or nine to eleven, you will have one or two weekly classes, consisting of one hour or an hour and a half each. At eleven or twelve, when you reach the in-termediate stage, you should take at least three weekly classes of one and one-half hours. In your fourth year of training, you will probably begin elementary toe work, if you are a girl, and take an extra boy's class, if you are a boy. When you reach the advanced classes—approximately five years after you've begun study—you should be having six lessons a week. This schedule will go on through your life as a dancer.

Most professional dancers are ready to join a corps de ballet at the age of sixteen or seventeen. From that point on, a dancer's rise through the company ranks is unpredictable, but generally two or three years will be spent on each rung of the ladder.

Considering the amount of time you will be spending in school, you will want

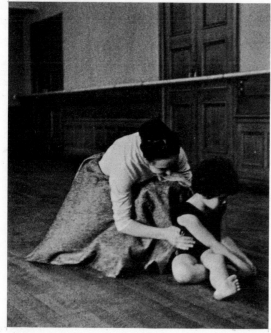

A student is shown how to move her body

André Eglevsky directs young pupil's steps

naturally to enroll in one that is near your home. This will save time and the money that would be spent on transportation. However, if the choice depends on an extra half hour on the bus for a superior teacher, by all means choose the teacher rather than save the time. Your teachers will be the most prominent influences in your development as a dancer, and you must choose wisely.

Finding a good school—and a good teacher—is fairly simple in a large city but not so easy in a small town. New York City, or Chicago, or San Francisco is, of course, ideal for dance study. These are also the cities that an aspiring dancer will go to when she hopes to join a professional company. There are several professional ballet schools in New York—the School of American Ballet, the American Ballet Theatre School, the Ballet Russe de Monte Carlo School of Ballet, and the Metropolitan Opera Ballet School, to name a few. Qualified students of the company schools have first chance at the jobs in their home companies.

Chicago has its Allegro School of Ballet, Stone-Cameron School, Edna Mc-Rae School of the Dance, and Ellis-Du Boulay School of Ballet, among others; Pasadena, its Le Mone Ballet Center; and San Francisco its Pacific Ballet Company, and San Francisco Ballet School. There are, for that matter, many excellent schools throughout the United States. But choosing the right one for you is so important to your development

Moving in response to rhythm is one of the first things a young dancer must learn to do

as a dancer that it is worth considerable time and thought before you make a decision. Together, you and your teacher are going to build a dancer's body and dancer's legs. This kind of muscle construction and development is unlike any other, so your training must be correct and consistent.

Just as your family may rely on one family doctor for many years, you will find it advisable to stay with one teacher during your beginning and intermediate training. The doctor is familiar with you and your medical history in the same way that your first teacher knows your physical capacities and physical needs. A good instructor will work with each pupil's individual problems. You will be taught how to minimize flaws in

body construction, such as too-short legs or arms, and how to make the most of natural assets, like a long neck and graceful hands.

There are several steps that you can take to insure getting proper instruction. First, check the phone book to learn the names of schools and teachers in your area, or in the largest city near your town. Then consult *Dance Magazine* or *Dance News* for listings in their school directories. You can also write to these periodicals (they are trade publications and all professional dancers read them). They will not recommend one teacher over another but they are available for further information. Anatole Chujoy's *Dance Encyclopedia* is probably owned by your local library and

Practice clothes should always be very simple

you can get additional background on individual teachers from this source.

Once you have located the names and addresses of nearby schools and teachers, you can narrow your choice.

Perhaps you have a favorite ballerina or a favorite company. Write to them telling them what is available in your area and asking for advice. If a fine ballet company recommends a teacher, you may rest assured that the teacher's training, experience, and reputation are all good.

When you have gathered together as much information as you can, go to the school that seems the best choice and visit a class or two. You won't be able to tell much technically about what is going on, but at least you will get an idea of what the teacher is like and what you may expect. If you are admitted to the school, you will be spending several years there, so have a long look before you sign up.

You will also have an interview with your prospective teacher, who will then decide whether or not to accept you.

In your early training, whether your teacher is male or female doesn't matter very much. But later on, for "finishing" —that is, polishing and refining your technique—you should study with a teacher of your own sex.

Only a woman really knows the peculiarities of dancing on pointe. Dancing on the tips of her toes emphasizes the feeling of weightlessness and airy grace that a ballerina must achieve, and a woman teacher with considerable experience is best qualified to instruct the young female dancer in the delicacy and precision of pointe work.

In the same manner, only a man can truly understand the strengths a male dancer must develop and the particular problems of partnering a ballerina. The technique of the male dancer must be every bit as good as is the female's, and in addition he must excel in elevation (leaps) and must have the ability and timing necessary to catch the ballerina in full flight, to give her steady support in the controlled adagio movements, and to lift her seemingly without effort.

As we said earlier, you should start your training when you are eight or nine years old, but there is no set rule about this. One school may admit students according to age, while another will base admission on physical development. It generally takes about eight years to build a dancer, and you should remember that most dancers are working professionally by the time they are in their late teens. There are exceptions to the rule of starting training early. Allegra Kent, for example, did not begin until she was almost twelve. But such examples *are* exceptions and, if at all

The mirrored walls of the studio hold the images of dancers who have worked before them

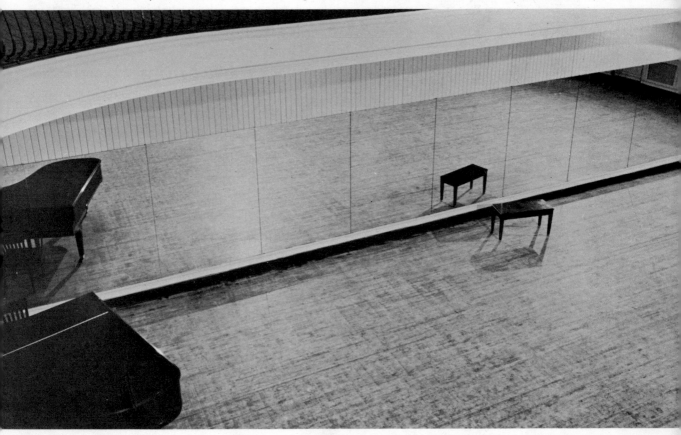

possible, your lessons should begin whenever your body is sufficiently developed.

Boys tend to begin lessons later than girls. This is too bad, as it means that they will have to work very hard when they finally do start and often have to support themselves while they are getting their training.

Unfortunately, in this country boys are sometimes considered sissies if they show an interest in dancing. In other parts of the world this is not so. When the great choreographer George Balanchine was a boy in Russia, his admittance to the Imperial School of Ballet pleased his parents as much as if he had been accepted at the Imperial Military Academy to which he had also applied.

One problem the boy dancer faces is that building dance muscles often conflicts with his taking part in competitive sports. To repeat, a ballet dancer's muscles are especially developed for ballet dancing. Another kind of athletics could exaggerate one set of muscles and spoil the dancer's body for dancing. Another factor is that, once a boy has become a serious dance student, his free time is likely to be taken up with classes, leaving him few spare hours even for individual sports such as golf or tennis.

Hopefully, as more and more Americans are educated about ballet and about dance in general, and the extremely high degree of skill and athleticism that they require, we will come to regard a career as a professional male dancer with the respect it deserves.

You and the teacher work together to build that unique instrument, a dancer's body

Because good male dancers are scarce in this country, ballet schools are eager to accept young boys who show promise and they often offer scholarships. So if you are a boy with the impulse to be a dancer, it is much to your advantage to begin training early.

If you start classes at the age of eight or nine, it will be almost impossible to tell immediately whether or not you have the makings of a ballet dancer. Your teachers can see that your legs and back are straight, that your foot shows some arch, that your body is flexible, and that you're not too fat, but it isn't until you are twelve or fourteen that your body begins to take its final physical shape.

One mistake that many parents make is to decide that their child is a born dancer simply because he or she responds to music and "dances" to it. It is

a rare child who doesn't. A child should always be looked at by a qualified teacher, who will at least be able to tell if the basic body structure is there to work with.

By the age of thirteen or so, when a girl's baby fat begins to melt away and hips and breasts appear, a teacher can then decide if she is ever going to have a dancer's body and the grace and pliancy necessary to a professional.

If you are one whose physique does not promise well for dance, your teacher will probably tell you so—gently but firmly. If your heart has been set on a place in the corps de ballet or a soloist's roles, this will be hard to take. But try not to be too discouraged. There are still many doors open to you. These will be discussed at the close of Chapter Three.

If, for brief periods, it is impossible for you to take the number of weekly

Mothers and very young visitors watch danseur noble André Eglevsky. Choosing a teacher is one of the most important decisions you and your parents make together

classes indicated at your level of training, then you may have to practice at home. Many teachers do not approve of this, so be sure to consult your teacher before you undertake solitary practice. It will only be a waste of time or set you back if you develop bad habits on your own that your teachers will have to undo. If your teacher approves, however, there is an excellent book on technique called *The Classic Ballet* (by Muriel Stuart of the School of American Ballet) that may help you study at home.

When will you be able to dance on pointe? This is a very important question and one that has been given much thought by professionals. If you begin working on toe too soon, you can do damage to your feet that nothing will be able to correct. If your bones are still too young and soft, if your posture is not correct, and if the supporting muscles in your legs and back are not sufficiently developed, your joints can become enlarged and your feet deformed. This can cause great pain and ruin your feet.

Since you've already gone to a good deal of trouble to select the right teacher, it's only sensible to do exactly what he or she says about pointe. A good instructor will have given the matter serious consideration and will have been preparing you for pointe work all during your early training.

And don't sneak into a pair of toe shoes and hobble around in them in the privacy of your room. It's a great temptation, but resist it. It cannot be said

Teacher and pupil and onlooking students all share the fun of a well-performed jump

The first time you perform in public will be a serious, but tremendously exciting, event

too often that you could seriously hurt your chances of becoming a dancer by anticipating the time for pointe work.

In time, you may "outgrow" a teacher. When this happens, both of you will sense it. But don't change for change's sake, because your best friend is changing, or because you have become temporarily bored with what you are doing. A good teacher can give you a wealth of dance experience, so spend as many years in his or her classroom as it takes to assure you of a sound basic technique.

A ballet classroom, like the backstage area of an empty theater, is part of the real glamour in ballet. You may not think so when you first see one. A big room, three plain walls with a wooden bar—called the barre—running around them, a large mirror on the fourth wall, a bare floor, and a piano in a corner. In summer it will probably be very hot, and in winter, clammy cold. But this room, like the theater, has a strong personality. If you look hard, you can almost see in the mirror the ghosts of earnest students working painstakingly at the barre. The very bareness of the room hints at the seriousness and dedication of the work that has been done there. This bareness, simplicity, *leanness*—like the leanness of the dancer's body—is really the essence of glamour

Scenery and costumes are part of recitals

your hair. You are striving for the long, clean line of the dancer, so distracting clothes are out of place. Practice clothes should be as simple as possible, for your teacher must be able to see what each part of your body is doing.

Girls' leotards come in a variety of colors, styles, and fabrics. Some have short skirts which may help give you a sense of flowing motion, but the great majority of teachers prefer that you wear one without a skirt. The most popular color is black; however, if you want something brighter you can certainly have it. Tights are generally wool, most often black or flesh pink for girls, and ankle length. Since the development of stretch fabrics, many dancers prefer this type of material for their tights: it clings and bounces back into shape. Many colors are available, either for a change or because you just happen to like them. Some people wear tights with feet, but the feet tend to wear out quickly and socks can be worn with the ankle-length tights and practice shoes. The latter are made of soft, pliable leather and require a narrow elastic strap over the instep which you will sew on from elastic you buy by the yard.

Boys wear sweaters, jerseys, or T-shirts with black or colored ankle-length tights, socks, and practice shoes. Their shoes, too, require the elastic.

Have you ever watched a tennis player warm up for a match? He often wears a sweater or jacket over his regular playing clothes until he has hit enough balls to warm up his muscles. It is the same

in dance. For out of these surroundings, this atmosphere, will come the beautiful music, the lush costumes, the splendid scenery, and the glorious dancing of the performance.

Later, after you have come here often and joined the ghosts in the mirror, you will feel a special little thrill when you enter this room. You are a part of this world and this is yours. It belongs only to the special people who are willing, longing, to work and work and work to be a part of it.

When you go to school, you will take with you a bag containing a leotard, tights, practice shoes, a towel and, if you are a girl, something to tie back

25

You must practice every day at the barre

En attitude, *with the barre as your support*

You get tired; you make yourself continue

You learn how to stretch further each time

with the dancer. Keeping warm is one of the dancer's most persistent problems, and dance studios are often cold. You can wear an extra sweater during the first few exercises, and woolen tights when you are beginning practice, or if you have to wait idly during a class. The sleeves of an old sweater are often used for this purpose. Just cut them off at the arm holes and roll them on to cover the leg from the ankles to the tops of the thighs.

For girls: never wear a belt. It will constrict your movement and could injure your partner during lifts in an adagio class. If you must show off your small waist, tie an attractive scarf around it.

Tie something around your hair to keep it back, or pin it firmly in place. Even if it's cut short, you'll probably have straggly ends sticking to your forehead after the first fifteen minutes. It will not only get in your way, but is

This is a class at the School of American Ballet. In the background, Mme. Felia Doubrovska

unattractive and messy-looking.

All students should bring a towel with them. You may be cold at the start, but after a few hard exercises at the barre, you'll need to wipe the sweat off your brow.

When you begin working on pointe, the fit and care of your toe shoes is of prime importance. Toe shoes are made like baby shoes and—like your soft ballet slippers—they have no rights or lefts. This is because "no footedness" gives

better balance and a straighter point. Keep them that way by changing them from foot to foot every few times you wear them.

Never buy ballet shoes to grow into. They must fit snugly. You will sew on your own ribbons. You will best know at what place along the side of the shoe to attach them so that they'll give you the most security. Your teacher will show you how to tie the ribbons just tightly enough to keep the toe shoe

One purpose of adagio classes is to teach boys and girls to work with each other as partners

When you audition, you must be as prepared as you would be for an actual performance

firmly in place and permit you to dance comfortably, without interfering with circulation. Many dancers also use a piece of elastic running from the back of the heel around the ankle to keep the heels of the shoes from slipping down. This too must be sewn on at home, if your teacher approves of it. Some teachers do not approve its use.

For performances, female dancers often use a water-soluble glue to paste the heels of their shoes to their tights. Male dancers do the same with their soft shoes. Then they don't have to use elastic, which interferes with the line of foot and leg.

Practice toe shoes are almost always pink, and are worn with pink tights. This gives the longest line to the leg and foot and adds to the illusion that the dancer is floating.

To cushion your toes in their boxed shoes, wrap the toes in pieces of lamb's wool. Some dancers use a scrap of fur, some foam rubber. You can start with lamb's wool—the most commonly used— and experiment as you become more expert on pointe.

Classes will be held in much the same manner wherever you go. A class of an hour and a half is divided into three parts: exercises at the barre (*à la barre*, in French), exercises in the center of the room (*au centre, adagio*), and turns and jumps (*allegro*). You will spend forty minutes or so at the barre and your "center practice" (a technical term) takes the remaining time.

As you become more advanced, some of this time will be devoted to jumps for the boys and toe work for the girls. Adagio classes, in which the boys partner the girls and both learn to execute the slow, controlled movements of the classical *pas de deux*, are also given for advanced pupils.

During the time spent working in the center of the room, you will do again many of the exercises you did at the barre, only this time you will have no support to hold onto. Your teacher will also give you a series of steps woven into a pattern, as they might be in an actual ballet. You will do these until you have learned them and can perform them correctly, then you will work on another series.

You will note that the class builds from the simpler barre work through adagio (in the center) to allegro (also in the center), which requires the maximum degree of pliability—i.e. when the body is warmest.

You will do the same barre exercises over and over, every day without fail, to the end of your days as a dancer. While it may not sound like it, this is one of the comforts of being a ballet dancer. Although the exercises may become dull and dreary after a while, you know that our prima ballerina assoluta Maria Tallchief and Britain's Margot Fonteyn have to do them too. Even one day without practice for the greatest dancer can lead to stiffened muscles and possible strain. And, as with many tasks you have to grit your teeth to do, there is satisfaction just in having done them.

29

The classroom is no place for giggles or chatter. If your teacher doesn't make you be quiet, your classmates probably will. This is a workroom and everyone knows it. If you keep on being silly, your teacher will ask you to leave. This is serious punishment for an aspiring ballet dancer who needs all the practice time she can get. So do your exercises diligently and study your reflection in the mirror only to see what you are doing and how and where you should correct flaws. You can gossip after class, in the dressing room.

After practice, you should take a warm shower or at least cool down before leaving school. You will have many aches and pains, not only at the begin-ning but all through your career. Often when you use a new muscle or stretch one a little bit farther, it's going to hurt. Get used to it. There isn't much to do but go home and soak in a warm bath with Epsom salts. And practice just as hard the next day or your progress will be lost.

Remember that, like an athlete, you are in training, and the rules of diet apply to you just as they do to a football or baseball player. Only your activity is not seasonal. You must train practically all the time.

Diet is simple. Meats and vegetables. Steaks and salad. Not much in the way of starchy foods, like potatoes, bread, or beans, or sweets. They might make

Before curtain time you finish getting ready

You make necessary last-minute adjustments

you gain weight and it is most important that you stay slim—even a bit underweight, if this doesn't make you weak. You must be strong, but light enough to be lifted easily by your partner and slender enough to look like a ballet dancer. Dancers are enormously critical of their own—and everyone else's—bodies, and can spot an extra ounce of flesh at twenty paces. They will also tell you about it in no uncertain terms so, for the sake of your feelings, watch out.

An occasional candy bar is fine if you need extra energy, but just because you're wildly hungry after class, don't go to pieces at the soda fountain. As a matter of fact, you will be hungry a lot of the time. Eat, but eat the right things.

Smoking is as bad for the dancer as it is for the athlete. It will shorten your breath, and you'll need all the breath you can get.

Rest is essential. Eight hours of sleep is considered the minimum amount a non-athletic adult requires, but you are an active young dancer who may need ten hours or more. Ask your teacher and your family doctor, and heed their advice. Your parents will undoubtedly insist that you get to bed early anyway, but remember that they are doing you a favor and comply willingly.

There will probably be times when the combination of classes, practice, and homework will make you feel tense and

Waiting plays a part in every dancer's life

Be sure to keep your working muscles warm

A good teacher demonstrates for his students what movements he wants them to perform

keyed up. At these times it will be helpful if you find some quiet activity to help you relax and unwind. A leisurely walk might do it, or perhaps a swim at the Y. It will help your parents to help you if they know that sometimes you do feel strained. Your mother or father could give you a back-rub or massage—excellent remedies for weary muscles.

Competitive athletics, with the exception of swimming, are not recommended for girl dancers. Some sports tend to develop muscles and attitudes that a dancer doesn't need and doesn't want. Swimming is relaxing and eases tension, and the muscles it requires won't conflict with a ballet body.

Boys needn't be quite as careful, because they need strength as well as grace and some forms of athletics can increase their stamina and endurance. Again, the teacher should be consulted.

There are a good many scholarships available at professional ballet schools. Some provide for a part of a student's tuition, some for all of it, and some even give the student an allowance for living expenses. The cost of ballet lessons varies somewhat from school to school, but you will generally have to pay between $1.50 and $3.00 per class. The more classes you take each week, the lower the rates.

The best way to find out about rates and scholarships at different schools is to consult *Dance Magazine* for names and addresses and then write to the schools, inquiring directly.

When you have graduated from beginner's classes, it is time to think about how you can acquire some real stage experience. It is an old adage that you can't get a job without experience, and you can't get experience without a job, so it is vitally important to you to make as many public dancing appearances as you can while you are studying.

A major aid in giving the prospective dancer a chance to perform is the regional ballet company. Regional companies are not professional. They are basically student companies, sponsored by civic groups and including the students of several schools and teachers in the

Scott Douglas, Nora Kaye, John Kriza and Jillana work together in rehearsing for a ballet

area. Frequently they have a professional guest director, choreographer, or soloist, and they give two concerts a year.
The concerts often include ballets from
the standard repertory and sometimes a
work especially commissioned for the
company. This is much more "professional" than the regular dancing school
recital and gives the student an invaluable taste of real performance.

There are about 175 of these regional
companies in the United States today.
A company may have from fifteen to
forty dancers, and their ages will range
from thirteen to eighteen. If at all possible, try to join one. Their standards
are high, and quite a few dancers have
gone on to join a professional company
after some experience with a regional
group. Make sure that you take the
same care in choosing a company as you
did in choosing your teacher. Also be
certain to have your teacher's approval.

If your goal is to dance with a professional ballet company, you may think
that your education outside the studio
is really not very important. This is not
so. No one can become an artist with
only technical knowledge. All forms of
creative endeavor demand that you
know as much about other art forms
and man's history as possible. One of
the biggest favors you can do for yourself is to work just as hard in school as
you would at the barre.

In New York City, for instance, there
are three schools which admit only pre-
professional and professional students

*Great professionals work just as seriously
in a ballet studio as do the young novices*

and students of the arts: the Professional Children's School, the High School
of Performing Arts, and the High
School of Music and Art.

In many other cities, however, special
academic schools are not available, and
you will be attending your own local
high school. If you succeed in becoming
a professional dancer, this will probably
be terminal education for you, your
last formal academic schooling, so make
the most of it. Whether you choose to
study well or not depends on you, but it
would be a big mistake merely to get by
in your classes.

There are particular areas of study
that will be most helpful. English is a
must. In addition to the grammar that
you study because you want to be an
educated person in your speech as well
as in your movements, you will read

plays, analyze characters that you may one day dance in a ballet, write compositions—perhaps about your favorite subject, dancing—gain sensivity through reading fine poetry, novels, and plays, and achieve poise through reading aloud to your class.

History will give you a sense of the past, an understanding of a situation in another time and place—basic requirements for creating character in a part. History will tell you how people dressed in other times, how they lived, and give you a feeling of their mood and style.

Mathematics teaches you to count, and you will certainly need to count when you learn a ballet. You will have to count how many beats it takes you to get from here to there many, many times. Geometry may be of some help in working out floor patterns, as Regina J. Woody has suggested in her *Young Dancer's Career Book*. Plane and space relationships are the tools of the choreographer. Always, when a subject gives you trouble in school, apply it to your dancing and notice how it will come alive.

Anything you learn about art in any form will be invaluable to you. You should soak up material on form, color, line, structure. Try to relate what you are learning in another field to what you are doing in dance.

Music, music, music! Whatever musical experience you can acquire is not only good for you but a necessity. If you can play an instrument, so much the better, but in any case listen to as much music as you can, study its form, and read about the people who compose and perform it. A dancer must have a sense of rhythm, of musical line, of beat, and of feeling. These things are absolutely essential.

It will be helpful if you can join a drama club in your school. While dancers don't have to take acting lessons, act they must, and any time spent in actual performance, whether as an amateur or professional, will add to your practical experience.

Perhaps you will have a ballet teacher who often refers to dancers of the present and past, to choreographers, to the origin of steps. This sort of talk will help educate you in the life of ballet. But, for the most part, your education in the history of ballet will come because you seek it out. You are reading this book because you want to know what it's like to be a dance student and a dancer. So you will read many others to find out what it was like for other dancers in other times. You will find a list of ballet books at the end of this one. Learning about ballet—about the magic of Pavlova and the genius of Fokine, for example—will be almost as much a part of your life as your hours at the barre.

You will learn because you ask questions, because you read about the past, because you keep up with current news in the dance world. Little by little, you will find yourself acquiring a self-taught course in ballet history. The knowledge you have gained will encourage you, inspire you to do better, and add to that very special sense of your ballet world.

Your first goal is to work in the corps de ballet, dancing in support of fine soloists

Chapter Three

YOUR FIRST JOB

*Now that you are ready for professional
work, how do you get a job? What
will your life be like backstage?*

If you are set on becoming a classic ballerina when you are ready to go to work, you will try to become a member of the corps de ballet of a national ballet company.

Let's say that you are seventeen and have been studying ballet for eight years. Your technique is strong and your teacher says it's time for you to seek professional experience. How do you go about this?

Hopefully, you've already performed in recitals where you live, and at other local functions. If you have, you will be able to answer the inevitable question asked at auditions: "What experience have you had?"

Perhaps you are a member of a regional company. If so, you might even be "discovered." George Balanchine and

Diana Adams recently toured the country's regional companies in a search for promising young dancers who deserved scholarships at the School of American Ballet or who could become apprentices to the New York City Ballet.

Before you decide to look for a job, discuss the matter thoroughly with your family and teacher. If they agree that you should go, chances are that you'll head for New York, where the three major national companies—Ballet Russe de Monte Carlo, American Ballet Theatre, and the New York City Ballet—are located. Or you may go to Chicago or San Francisco.

The best thing to do when you arrive is enroll immediately in the school of the company you prefer. If you cannot get a scholarship, you ought to have enough

Your ability to learn quickly is important

The judges note many aspects of your skill

money for a few months' lessons. You will be working on your technique while you look for a job. Also—and most important—the teachers and directors of the company are always looking among their own pupils for new dancers.

After you've picked your school, try to find a room or small apartment to share with another dancer, or with a member of your family who has come to stay with you. The school will have a bulletin board with news of auditions, and often with announcements of rooms or apartments to share. You should also buy the dance trade magazines—*Dance Magazine, Dance News*. They will keep you informed about what's going on in your field.

Once you're established in the city, it is a matter of talent, hard work, luck—or a combination of all three—that will decide your future in ballet. Your teacher will analyze your chances quite honestly, and will probably make sugges-

tions as to how you should proceed. You may have to earn a living while you wait for a break. The teachers can advise you if it would be better to look for another kind of dance job or for non-theatrical work that would still allow time for classes and auditions.

When the time comes for you to go to an audition, you will want to be prepared. You should take—or wear under your outer clothes—tights, leotard, toe shoes for girls, and maybe an extra sweater. In other words, just about what you would normally wear for class. Keep the colors quiet and be sure that you are well groomed. While you don't have to be beautiful, your personal appearance does count.

You and other applicants will probably be asked to line up on stage or in a rehearsal studio. The director or choreographer will then give you a series of steps to execute. He not only wants to see what talent and ability you have,

If you are asked to do a solo variation, that is the time to show off your own specialties

but also how quickly you learn. You may be asked to do a solo variation of your own, so it is best to have something prepared and to bring your music with you. If you are very good at fouettés, for example, this is the time to show them off.

You will either be eliminated or asked to do some more complex routine. Perhaps—after you've been through this process many times, worked very hard, and gotten thoroughly discouraged—just perhaps you will be the one who gets the job.

What will your new life be like in the corps de ballet? Well, first you will join AGMA, the American Guild of Musical Artists. Your initiation fee and dues will be determined by the salary you earn on your first job. You'll probably pay between $25 and $100 initiation fee and about $8 quarterly in dues. AGMA sets your minimum wage, the number of hours you may be required to re-

hearse, and guarantees that some of your travel expenses will be paid by the company.

If you are joining a resident company during its season at home, first you'll be shown around your theater. A place will be assigned to you at one of the long, brightly lighted dressing tables in the corps' dressing room. You'll be told about the number of pairs of toe shoes that will be supplied by the company, where to keep them, and where to hang your things.

The ballet mistress will tell you what make-up you will need. Get a plastic tray with divided sections for hairpins, nets, safety pins, eyebrow pencils, sponges. You'll need hair spray, towels, cotton, tissues, and cold cream.

Practice clothes are kept in the theater for the classes that you'll be taking every day, and for rehearsals. The ballet mistress will cast you and teach you your parts.

George Balanchine rehearses Violette Verdy and members of the corps de ballet in steps for Raymonda. *As you progress in the corps, you will be assigned roles in many ballets*

Depending on your ability, how quickly you learn, and the company's needs, you will start in one, two, or more ballets, generally in very small roles. As you work and rehearse with the company, you'll learn more and more of the repertoire. Watching the others will help. Dancers usually develop very good eyes for steps and routines, and especially for the fine points of performance.

Let's take a look at the schedule of your first day of performance. There are four ballets on the program, but you are appearing only in the second one, *Firebird*. You are going to be one of the monsters.

The day begins with your regular ten o'clock class at school. You have moved from the Advanced to the Professional group, so even in school you are working with the stars of the company. This alone would be enough to excite you, but you have the additional knowledge that tonight you are actually going to dance *on stage*.

After class, you have lunch at a drug store with an older member of the corps, then go to the theater for a costume fitting. There is a monster costume that fits you, so no alterations need be made. Next comes a run-through of your part with the ballet mistress and a boy who is also joining the cast for the first time. You go over it again and again, for when the stage is dark and only the colored lights are on, you realize everything will look different. You must make your entrances and exits on time and from the right wings, just the same.

You needn't worry too much; everyone wants the performance to go smoothly so that, if you make a mistake, the more experienced dancers will help prod you through. But you must certainly try to be as prepared and perfect as possible, even if your part is small.

By now it is late afternoon and you've already had a very active day. Nerves permitting, you curl up in a quiet corner for a short rest. Surprisingly, you fall asleep for a bit. When you wake up it's almost six, and the rest of the company is beginning to arrive. You want something to eat and you are glad that you are not in the first ballet. This way, you'll have time to eat and digest before performance. You run around the corner to the delicatessen for a roast beef sandwich and some yogurt to take out.

Back in the theater, you eat your "supper" and then do your make-up. Actually, to be a monster you don't need much make-up because your costume covers almost all of you. But it makes you feel more at home to go through the routine, so you put on base, eye shadow and rouge, and draw your ballet eyes— long black lines on upper and lower lids that extend far out to the sides. You also pin your hair back in a bun and make it doubly secure with a net, more pins, and hair spray. Now at least you look like a ballerina.

Most of the corps is doing the same thing. They want to be made up by seven so that they can take the evening class in the theater.

After class, everyone appearing in

The master choreographer inspires the dancer

Once you are accepted in a corps de ballet, you will take classes with the stars

the very first ballet rushes around the dressing room freshening make-up and getting changed. In costume, the dancers go on stage to practice by themselves before curtain time. Still in your practice clothes, you join them and once again go over your part. The stage manager calls "On stage!" for the first ballet.

Suddenly it seems as if all the time has rushed by and you will never make your own entrance. You fly to the dressing room and into your costume, arriving breathless and shaky in the wings seven minutes later. You watch the rest of the first ballet, taking care to keep out of the way of the dancers as they leap on and off stage. But you can't really keep your mind on the performance. After all,

in a few minutes *you* will be out *there!*

Then the waiting is over. "On stage for *Firebird!*" says a voice. The curtain is up. There is the Prince and there the glittering Firebird herself. The monsters are assembling in the wings. In a sudden panic you search for the one you must follow. Then, a last whispered "Good luck," the familiar music, and you are on stage, leaping and whirling in the bright, wild lights.

Everything disappears—your fear, nervousness, worry over the steps—everything but the music, the lights, and the other dancers. You do what you have been taught without thinking and—miracle of miracles—without falling or losing your place. Much too soon, you are back in the wings again.

Nina Novak and Irina Borowska practice on stage with other members of the Ballet Russe

You might first be assigned a part in the corps of a youthful ballet like Graduation Ball

"I did it! I did it!" Over and over the phrase runs through your dazzled head. On you go again, to bow in the company curtain call and hear the lovely applause. There will never be another moment quite like this. You are a ballet dancer at last.

You have now been working, in one way or another, for nearly thirteen hours. From now on, your days will pass in much the same way, with the theater a second home, the center of your ballet world.

It has been said that a ballet company is only as good as its corps de ballet. Certainly, without a strong, disciplined corps everything will look ragged and sloppy. A member of the corps may not yet be an artist, but her technique is often as strong as the ballerina's. Whether she graduates to a higher rank will depend on her growth as a person and as a dancer, and on her own drive and ambition.

The corps de ballet can also be the proving ground for an ambitious young dancer. Here you will be trained, disciplined, taught the repertoire, shown the

Your dressing table will hold the conglomeration of accessories that your new job requires

Melissa Hayden completely transforms her features for a character role in The Cage

Allegra Kent's street make-up is very light. Here her part takes more lipstick, eye-lines

45

In costume backstage, you wait to go on

There are often some anxious last moments

meaning of style. Most important, you will be seen. How rapidly you advance depends on the same factors you encountered when you were looking for work. Mostly it depends on those individual qualities that make up *you*.

Just because you have a job in a company, this is no time to let down, to take it easy in class or skip one every so often. Remember that the classrooms and studios are overflowing with eager young dancers like you. They are just waiting for an opening with *your* company, perhaps your own place, should you fall down on the job. The vision of the ballet mistress, the directors and the choreographers is very sharp. They can easily tell if you are not improving or if you are falling behind.

In dance, you cannot stand still figuratively any more than you do literally. Just to stay where you are requires your best efforts every day. And to advance, you must constantly work at the very peak of your form.

But what of the students of dance who are less fortunate than you? Must those who do not make the grade in classical

46

You keep practicing backstage until the curtain time for your first actual performance

ballet give up all hope of working in the dance field?

This, unfortunately, is a question every prospective dancer should think about and be able to answer. If it has been his or her life-long ambition to dance professionally in ballet, the decision to give it up will be very painful. But it may be necessary.

There may be several reasons for this decision. It could be that the student's physical characteristics have not developed suitably. There are corrective exercises that can be taken, but it's possible

that they won't work, or that some flaw —such as too short legs—makes it impossible for the prospective dancer to dance ballet professionally.

It could be a question of technical ability. The teachers may decide that a student's progress has not been sufficient or sufficiently rapid.

Or it could be that the young dancer herself has seriously examined her motives and personality and decided that she was not cut out for the extreme discipline and dedicated life of the ballet dancer.

Teaching ballet might be the answer for you. If your technique is strong, your awareness of physical qualities and musical ability good, and if you like children and can communicate easily with them, teaching could be a very rewarding career. In that case, you would probably continue your training, but with specific emphasis on qualities you need to achieve your new goal.

If you are interested in teaching and in working with groups, you might consider a career in dance therapy. This has been proven to be of great value to handicapped children and adults, and to patients with some mental disease. For work of this kind you need special training. Your local hospital can probably tell you with whom to get in touch to learn what instruction you must have for a career in dance therapy.

You may want to try another form of

And there you are, as you longed to be, dancing one of the swan-girls in the corps de ballet

theater, where your knowledge could be a tremendous asset. You might want to act, or to direct.

There are many other forms of dance to which you may be better suited either as a performer or teacher: acrobatic, tap, modern or interpretive, character, folk dancing, jazz, or ballroom adagio, to name a few. There are also a great many places where you may perform, aside from the ballet stage: musical com-

edy, night clubs, movies, the revue stage, and the concert stage. Any one of these dance outlets may interest you. The ballet training you have had will give you a strong base from which you can go on to specialize in the field you choose.

Perhaps you have become intrigued by dance notation and would like either to practice it or teach it to others. Or perhaps you are interested in choreography.

And do not forget the possibility that you may now wish to go on to college, either to get a degree in modern dance or to take up entirely new subjects. You can check the list of colleges offering dance as a major in *Dance Magazine*. If your library doesn't have this magazine in its files you may write directly (231 West 58th Street, New York City 19) enclosing your name and address, plus one dollar for their college list.

As you can see, if a career as a ballet dancer is not for you, this does not mean the end of your future in dance or dance theater. As always, your teacher's understanding of your body structure, temperament and assets will give a good indication of where your abilities can be put to the best possible use.

No matter which field appeals to you most, always remember that you have not lost through the time spent in the ballet studio. You have gained poise, grace and strength. Even if it has only made you a good balletomane—given you a greater understanding and appreciation of ballet—your early training will have been of great value.

49

The handsome American Ballet Theatre production of Bluebeard *was designed by Marcel Vértes*

Chapter Four

THE BALLET COMPANY

*You need to know the many types
of artist involved in a ballet company
and what each one contributes*

If you've been doing your homework outside the classroom, you should by now have a good idea of how many people it takes to make a ballet and what their roles are. So let's discuss here who these people are and what they do.

We have been talking mainly about dancing because dancing is, of course, your chief concern. But you will feel unprofessional indeed if you don't understand how a ballet company functions.

The structure of the organization may vary slightly from company to company, but generally the pattern is similar. First comes the company director. He is the administrator, the one who decides which artists will best complement each other and produce the best ballet. He brings together the choreographer, composer, set designer, and costume design-er. If he is wise and assembles the right combination of artists, they will work creatively together and their combined talents will make a fine ballet. Serge Diaghilev, who established the Ballets Russes in western Europe, was such a man. Dame Ninette de Valois of Britain's Royal Ballet is such a woman. Lincoln Kirstein of the New York City Ballet is such a man.

Before the choreographer—the man who designs the dance patterns of a ballet—enters the scene, there must be the ballet mistress or master, a sort of technical manager of the company. And there are also the teachers—those who teach the dancers their roles and give them their classes day after day in the theater.

Then comes the choreographer. He

51

Scenery must both decorate and add to the feeling of movement

Costumes must suit the personality of a part, but must also permit the dancer to move freely

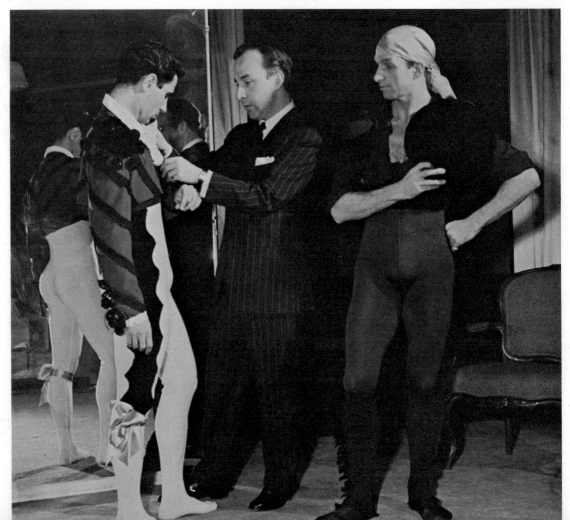

The costumes above are all from Figure in the Carpet, *and were designed by Karinska*

begins with an idea for a ballet. Perhaps he has read a story that he wants to set to music and dance, perhaps he has an original idea and wants to write his own scenario, or book. He works out his idea and begins to think of steps that will reveal the story. Or he may possibly listen to the music he has selected and invent large group patterns first, then work in the soloists' movements. In her biographical book, *Dance to the Piper*, Agnes de Mille says that she comes to the first rehearsal armed with notes and diagrams indicating the sequence and overall patterns and the type of movements that would be true to the characters in her ballet. After that, composition is done with the dancers themselves, in a rehearsal hall with a pianist and sometimes a phonograph. Sometimes dancers and their individual manner of moving will suggest an idea to the cho-

reographer. A soloist with the Ballet Russe is learning the part of a flirtatious Spanish girl. She beckons to her partner as she has been instructed to, then tilts her head coyly to one side. "That's good. Do that, keep that in," says Leon Danielian, the choreographer, enthusiastically.

When watching ballet, always remember that the choreographer must not only be concerned with pretty steps and exciting patterns, but with *motivation*. In a story ballet, if the dancers are not moving in a way in which the characters in the story would, the choreographer has not been successful. He is responsible for every movement that takes place on stage.

Keeping a large number of dancers moving in interesting groupings and designs is a major problem. The corps must be given controlled, flowing action that is fine in itself while also giving support to the story and to the soloists. If you sit in the balcony or mezzanine to watch a ballet, you can easily see the patterns take shape and change.

Remembering what has already been done is also difficult. Dancers often help the choreographer in this respect, because their bodies can frequently remember what his mind has temporarily forgotten. Dancers call this muscular memory. There are several systems of dance notation (Labanotation is the best known in this country) and choreographers may have codes of their own. Dancers are encouraged to study notation and, once they are trained, may add to their incomes by notating both new and existing ballets.

Many ballets are being noted down now so that they will not disappear with the passing of time and the unreliability of people's memories. If you want to know more about Labanotation and where you can study it, write to the Dance Notation Studio, 47 West 63rd Street, New York City.

A choreographer must have a great deal of experience as a dancer in addition to his own talent as a dance designer. He must know the technical range of his dancers; he cannot ask them to do something that is physically impossible. He should have a knowledge

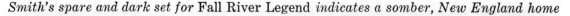

Smith's spare and dark set for Fall River Legend *indicates a somber, New England home*

Fancy Free *calls for the gay, light-hearted feeling of a night on the town in New York City*

Rodeo's *setting requires the atmosphere of wide open spaces and a pleasant ranch house*

In Graduation Ball, *the cadets and their girls romp against the elegance of a ballroom setting*

Giselle *shifts from the lively, pretty peasant girls shown above to the unearthly Wilis*

of music, painting and history, in addition to familiarity with the mechanics of the theater. And, of course, he must be able to communicate his ideas to the dancers. Some contemporary ballet choreographers whose names we know well are Antony Tudor, Eugene Loring, George Balanchine, Agnes de Mille, Jerome Robbins, and Frederick Ashton.

If the ballet is to be an "abstract" ballet—without a plot or characters, just dance to music—then the choreographer works with his choice of music and what it suggests to him.

Much ballet music is taken from the classics. Sometimes bits and pieces from several compositions are blended together by the choreographer and an arranger. But there are also many new scores that are commissioned—that is, assigned—from a composer for a new ballet. In that case, the composer and choreographer meet to discuss the plot, the division of plot into scenes, the background of the story, atmosphere and character of the plot. The composer needs to know as much as he can about

the situation which he is going to translate into music. His score, like the choreography, must suit the motivation and action of the characters. In Stravinsky's *Firebird* you can hear as well as see the sharp, fluttering movements of the captured Firebird and the girlish, pretty dances of the Princess and her handmaidens. In Aaron Copland's score for Agnes de Mille's *Rodeo*, the bucking rhythm of the cowboys on imaginary broncs is established by the music.

The set designer works with the same material as the composer: the choreographer's idea. His scenery must be faithful to the background of the plot, its time and place, and the mood of the ballet. Sets may be very realistic, abstract, or merely give an illusion of a house, a castle, or a forest. Scenery must provide an atmosphere for the dancers to move through, such as the house and street in Oliver Smith's set for *Fall River Legend*, but the sets must not distract from the dancing itself.

As a dancer, you will have to learn to work with scenery and props. You can't go bumping into trees, crashing into a fountain, or tripping over furniture. If you are carrying a wand or a sword, you can't bash your partner on the head with it, unless it's in the plot. You'll have to learn to avoid collision with inanimate objects as well as with your fellow dancers.

You may not work with either set or costumes before actual performance and suddenly find yourself in completely unfamiliar surroundings. This could cause chaos and even be dangerous, so look at the sets as soon as you can and carefully note where your exits and entrances are and the objects to be avoided. There will be drawings of the sets available during rehearsals, but it will feel different when you're actually on stage.

The costume designer must solve other

Peter and the Wolf, *like a great many of the ballets for children, is highly stylized*

problems. He should make costumes that are not only attractive in their own right, but are also suitable to the story, in harmony with the scenery, and allow the dancer to move with complete freedom.

If a new ballet is to be presented and you are dancing in the opening performance, you'll naturally have a new costume of your own. But if you are only appearing in ballets from the standard repertoire, your costumes will have been worn by other dancers before you. Alterations, refurbishing, cleaning, pressing, and mending are taken care of by the wardrobe mistress and her assistants.

A conductor of a ballet orchestra works in a slightly different manner from a conductor of, say, a symphony orchestra. He must work with the dancers as well as with his musicians. Musical tempo (relative speed) and phrasing are all-important to the dancer, and the conductor must always be aware of the dancer's technical problems. If the tempo is too slow, for example, a series of turns could demand fantastic control of the dancer. Or a too-fast tempo could make already rapid jumps impossible.

Again, you should be so sure of your own art and your own actions that an unforeseeable problem—like a change in tempo or a too-tight costume—will not disturb you too much.

Lighting is another very important phase of a ballet's production. When you go to the theater you can see many different colored lights coming from the back of the theater, the sides of the

Peppermint Stick's dance, The Nutcracker

Nutcracker's *exciting Chinese Tea dance*

The Mouse King–fearsome-looking menace

stage, and the footlights. How these lights are used—in what combinations —can establish the mood of a story, and bad lighting can ruin an effect. A spotlight that keeps missing a performer can make him look ridiculous; dark, ominous lighting during a gay party scene would be confusing and wrong.

In order to give you a feeling of how these related arts are applied, try to imagine how you would stage and design the scenery for a ballet. Take a recording of a piece of music that you like —Ravel's *La Valse,* for instance. Listen to it carefully several times. Then, start-

ing with the choreographer, make yourself assume the roles of each artist in turn. How does the music make you feel? Is it slightly sad and haunting or gay and exuberant? How many dancers will you want? Will you focus most of the attention on the ensemble or on featured soloists? Will everyone always have a partner, or will the boys and girls dance separately occasionally?

Will you include a *pas de deux?* If you do, where will it come in the music? How will the girls be dressed? In toe shoes and romantic tutus, or in 1912 evening gowns and high heels? The

59

Production styles differ from company to company. This is Royal Ballet's Cinderella

will also get an idea of some of the problems that face the creators of ballet.

As a matter of fact, *La Valse* is in the repertoire of the New York City Ballet. Perhaps you can see it soon and compare their interpretation with your own.

The dancers who are cast in the principal roles will bring their own styles and interpretations to the performance, too. One ballerina may dance a brilliant, staccato Firebird, while another will give a more emotional feeling to the role.

Thus the making of a ballet is the fusing of many talents. If all goes well, the result is a production of lasting beauty and value.

Just as every individual has a unique personality, every creative artist has a style all his own. A major factor of the director's job is to see to it that all the individual styles assembled in his production will be in harmony with one another and not clash or conflict.

Style extends to the ballet company as a whole, as well as to its members. This special flavor that identifies one company is partially due to the national characteristics of its homeland. The outgoing, volatile Italians were noted for their speed and agility, while the French preferred a slower, more lyrical style that reflected their love of grace and elegance. The Russians adapted both types of manner and brought to them a highly theatrical sense as well as the vitality of their peasant folk dances. England added her faultless manners and a quality of gentleness combined with majesty and splendor.

boys? Perhaps they should wear tights and beautifully jeweled white jackets. Or maybe you see the ballet in modern dress, with the boys in elegant black dinner jackets.

Where will *La Valse* take place? In a beautiful ballroom with crystal chandeliers? Or on a terrace overlooking the Mediterranean? Is the lighting gay and bright, with lots of pinks and yellows, or is it moonlit and misty, with pale blues and whites?

You can play this game with any composition that you can dance to. You can make up a story, or take a familiar one and find music that would suit it. If you do this with some friends, each one working separately, you are likely to get several very different results. You

The Ballet Russe production of Rouge et Noir, *with set and costumes designed by Matisse*

The principal dancer has a personal style

The Royal Danish Ballet boasts a marvelous group of fine, strong, young male dancers. This is not to neglect the girls, who are also fine. The Danes have kept the light, quick style of the romantic era. Both Russian companies—the Bolshoi Ballet and the Leningrad Kirov Ballet—have exceptionally good male dancers and many of them. The Russian companies are very dramatic and athletic, and perform technical marvels, while the English Royal Ballet places emphasis on pure, perfect performance and the more romantic style.

Three major American national companies—the American Ballet Theatre, Ballet Russe de Monte Carlo, and the New York City Ballet—have quite distinct styles of their own. We have borrowed some traits from the Europeans, but Americans have many national characteristics and these can clearly be seen in our ballets.

One of the greatest influences in American ballet has been George Balanchine. At the time of Diaghilev's death, Balanchine was choreographer for his Ballets Russes. Balanchine then formed his own company, Les Ballets 1933, which was seen by a young American ballet enthusiast, Lincoln Kirstein.

Kirstein persuaded Balanchine to come to the United States and direct the School of American Ballet. He has been its director ever since the American Ballet was formed. Its dancers were students of the School. The following year, the company became the resident company of the Metropolitan Opera.

In 1938, Kirstein established a second company out of the School of American Ballet. It was called Ballet Caravan and was to be a showcase for American talent. One of the most important ballets it produced was Eugene Loring's *Billy the Kid*. This production has been said to mark the true beginning of American Ballet.

The two companies merged under the name of American Ballet Caravan in 1941, but disbanded the same year. Balanchine stayed on as director of the School and Kirstein went into the Army.

In 1946, he was out of the service and he and Balanchine founded another company, this one called Ballet Society and seen by subscription only. Word rapidly got around that exciting new things were happening with this group and it was finally opened to the general public.

In 1948, after years of trying to establish its permanent company, Balanchine's Ballet Society (the name he and Kirstein gave to their post-war ballet group), was asked by the city of New York to make its home in City Center and change its name to the New York

Five ballerinas and five different styles—Borowska, Tyven, Tallchief, Novak and Chouteau

City Ballet. Kirstein and Balanchine at last found a permanent home for their company.

What is Balanchine's style? It is called neoclassicism and is solidly based on pure classic dance. Some of his most impressive work has been in ballets with no plot and no characters, just closely interwoven, integrated music and dance. *Serenade* is one of these. He has created a new type of dancer: Balanchine's ballerina is long-limbed, slender, strong, and possessed of a magnificent technique. Simplicity in decor is a Balanchine trademark. His ballets often have no sets at all. However, his recent productions of *The Nutcracker* and *A Midsummer Night's Dream* are lavishly designed and costumed.

American Ballet Theatre, which was founded in 1939 and, since 1946, has been under the direction of Lucia Chase and designer Oliver Smith, has quite a different character from Balanchine's New York City Ballet. Its classical style has been chiefly influenced by the romantic English school, and particularly by Alicia Markova and Anton Dolin. Antony Tudor, who is British, has had the greatest effect on Ballet Theatre's development and is considered by many as the first real innovator since Michel Fokine. While his choreography is firmly rooted in traditional classic dance, he has introduced serious studies of character as opposed to the traditional fairy tales, and devised a new kind of emotionally revealing movement to tell them. His have been called "psychological ballets."

Igor Youskevitch—scene from **Red Poppy**

*Danielian, Danilova, Franklin—*Swan Lake

American Ballet Theatre's repertoire contains a wide variety of choreographic styles including works by Tudor, Balanchine, Frederick Ashton, Frederick Franklin, Jerome Robbins, Brigit Cullberg, William Dollar, Adolph Bolm, Michel Fokine, and Marius Petipa.

The Ballet Russe de Monte Carlo has been an American company since 1938, under the direction of Sergei J. Denham. It doesn't have a theater of its own—neither does Ballet Theatre—but flourishes as a touring company. Unlike the other two companies, Ballet Russe still believes in a star system, and over the years many of the most brilliant dance stars of our time have worked for the company. For many years prima ballerina assoluta Alexandra Danilova headed the roster, and some of the other

Alicia Alonso as she dances ethereal Giselle

great names associated with Ballet Russe include Leonide Massine, Alicia Markova, Frederic Franklin, Leon Danielian (Danielian is now doing choreography for the company and is a teacher at its school), Alicia Alonso, Igor Youskevitch, Ruthanna Boris, Mia Slavenska, Yvonne Chouteau, Maria Tallchief, Nina Novak, and George Zoritch. Novak and Zoritch are now the company's principal dancers.

Ballet Russe is high-spirited, emotional, and dramatic. It has a fairly standard repertoire and doesn't add new works too frequently, but its large audience loves its dancers just the same.

It is difficult to understand about such things as style and technique by reading about them. The most important thing is to see them at work. Fortunately for young people all over the country, we are now able to see our own fine companies on their tours, and also many of the foreign ones. The visits of the Europeans are in good measure thanks to the efforts of impresario Sol Hurok, who has brought, and continues to bring, the best in entertainment and culture from other lands for us to see. Other producers are also bringing foreign groups here, and the admiration inspired by these performers has been of great value to our own dancers.

So don't let your dance education come only from books and the classroom. Your appreciation and knowledge of your art will grow every time you see a performance. By all means, go to the ballet and go often.

The greatest sensation in 19th century ballet in America was Austrian Fanny Elssler

Chapter Five

BALLET'S PAST

*Where did ballet begin and how has
it grown as an art? Who are the people
who formed today's classic ballet?*

Now that you've taken a good look at what your life will be like in ballet school and in a ballet company today, it's time you explore the roots of ballet. You realize the importance of knowing as much as possible about the arts related to dancing. It is equally important to know the history of your own art.

Theatrical dancing has been known since the time of the ancient Greeks. They put on plays that combined pantomime with a chorus of dancers and singers. But this was primarily theater, with dance used to illustrate points in the drama. It was not ballet as we know it. (The word *ballet* comes from the Italian *ballare*, which means *to dance*.)

Throughout the Middle Ages, there were strolling companies of minstrels, clowns and acrobats, but their so-called "ballets" were really only unrelated entertaining dances, often performed in the streets when a crowd gathered.

The first performance we would call a ballet—that is, dancers in a stage area, with scenery, and an understandable story line, before a seated audience—was not presented until late in the 16th century. This was *Le Ballet Comique de la Reine*, or *The Comic Ballet of the Queen*. It was sponsored at the French court in 1581 by Catherine de Medici, the Queen Mother of France.

When Catherine came to France from Italy as the wife of Henry II, she missed the elaborate entertainments of the Italian court and soon sent for a troupe of actors, singers, and musicians. The Italian productions—not precisely ballet, but a mixture of speech, song, and dance

The court of Louis XIV at Versailles presented many ballets. The king himself took part

—had been very popular at the Italian courts and this popularity soon spread to France. One of Catherine's recruits was a fine violinist who called himself Beaujoyeux. He composed *Le Ballet Comique* and thus began a new era in dance. This ballet also marked the beginning of the corps de ballet. Until this time, court dancing had been a man's pastime with men playing all the parts, including those of women. After Beaujoyeux, ladies in the French court were at last permitted to take part.

Ballet soon became the favorite diversion of every European court rich enough to hire the entertainers.

In the time of Louis XIV, some eighty years after its first introduction in France, ballet was opened to the public —not just to the nobility. Louis loved dance and was a competent performer. He took part in many performances himself. Usually he played gods or kings.

In 1661, Louis established the National Academy of Music and Dance. Eight years later, he himself stopped dancing: he loved many aspects of gracious living, including good food, and had become too fat to continue as a performer. With Louis' absence from the entertainments, the court lost interest. Through the foundation of the Academy, however, Louis had helped assure a future for ballet. Instead of merely being a diversion for the nobility, it grew increasingly into an entertainment for the other classes. Ballets were presented in schools, at festivals, and in theaters, to growing audiences.

Although its form, a blending of music, story, scenery, costumes, and dance, resembled modern theatrical ballet, the ballet of the French court differed from the classic dancing we know today. Costumes were ornate, skirts long and heavy, masks were worn to suit the character the dancer was playing, and slippers had high heels. Imagine what it would be like to try to dance while wearing a heavily boned corset, a towering wig, a stifling mask, wide, swaying hoop skirts, and giddy high heels! The weight alone would probably bring you to your knees.

Much of the style of dance was based on the limitations the costumes imposed on the dancers. Elevation was impossible. At best, the dancers could move about slowly and gracefully, or do very simple steps and turns. Since the ladies' feet could not be seen, what was the point of intricate steps?

Choreographers, according to Arnold Haskell, resorted to wires and machinery to hoist the heavily-clad dancers into the air in order to get some feeling of elevation and lightness from them. Happily, out of this initial heaviness and immobility came the slow, elegant *adagio* style of ballet for which France has been famous ever since.

Pierre Beauchamp, who has been called the father of dancing masters, was a ballet master of the court and of the Academy. It was he who codified and

Costumes were very elaborate, skirts were long and heavy and slippers had high heels

The king loved to dance and quite often he took the part of the mythical god, Apollo

69

*The delicate-looking Taglioni personified
romance of the early nineteenth century*

defined the turned out-positions. His
dancers did not do the advanced turnout
that we know, but this was the start.

Jean Georges Noverre, a choreographer of the 18th century, was, at different times, ballet master of the courts of
France, Stuttgart, Vienna, and St. Petersburg, and at the Paris Opera. He
greatly advanced the drama in ballet
and was responsible for the introduction of the *ballet d'action*, or dramatic
ballet. His influence was extremely important in the introduction of costumes
that were shorter and less restricting.

He wrote extensively of his belief that
composer, choreographer, and designer
should all work together to create a
ballet.

Marie Camargo was the first dancer
to make drastic changes in ballet costume. La Camargo made her debut with
the Paris Opera ballet in 1726, when
she shocked and delighted the ballet public by shortening her skirts to above her
ankles and wearing flat-heeled slippers.
After that, wigs and masks began to
disappear and ballet dancing became
more active. A new style of dancing,

La Camargo was the first ballet dancer who
dared to shorten her skirts above the ankle

La Cachucha *was one of the many ballets
that Fanny Elssler introduced to the U.S.*

called *allegro* and made possible by the
less inhibiting costumes, was born.
Dancers were able to move about quickly and steps became more complicated.
With their masks off, dancers had to
show that they could act, too.

France remained the ballet center of
Europe until 1789, the time of the
French Revolution. One of the major
reasons for this was that Italy was divided into many principalities and had
many courts. It had no Paris, no single
court that was the center of power and
arbiter of taste. But with the coming of

the Revolution and the nobility's deci-
sive loss of power, classical ballet de-
clined in France. There was no longer
money from the aristocracy to support
the ballet, and many dancers went to
Russia, Italy, or the United States,
where they could continue practicing
their art.

In Italy, *allegro* dancing continued to
develop. *Allegro* means lively or joyous
in Italian, and this form of dance involved a precision of acrobatic technique and elevation that no one had ever
seen before. The new Italian ballerinas

Fokine, who revolutionized the traditions of ballet, was Diaghilev's choreographer

As the amorous duke Albrecht in Giselle, *Nijinsky danced "disguised" as a peasant*

leaped into their partners' open arms, and audiences were enchanted.

Early in the 19th century, Carlo Blasis, in Milan, refined and notated the technique of turnout, and established the exercises at the barre that ballet students have practiced ever since. In 1837, he founded the Academy of Dancing at Milan. The entrance requirements strongly resembled those of the great schools we know today. Pupils were not admitted before the age of eight, and girls were not admitted after twelve. (Boys could be as old as fourteen.)

What was happening in Russia during this time? From the reign of Peter the Great, in the last of the 17th and first of the 18th centuries, dance gained more and more of a place in Russia's culture. It was part of Peter's policy to westernize his country, borrowing the best in art, dress, and architecture from other lands. During his reign and those of the Empresses Anne, Elisabeth, and Catherine the Great who followed him, many visitors from abroad went to Russia to take advantage of that country's cultural awakening.

When the French Revolution made it impractical for artists to remain in Paris, the wealthy Russian court offered them a haven and an enthusiastic new

Nijinsky, with Karsavina, in his famous impersonation in Le Spectre de la Rose

audience eagerly awaited them.

The beginning of the 19th century saw a new phase of ballet evolve. This was the idealization of the fragile female—the great romantic period. An extraordinarily delicate-looking creature named Marie Taglioni was the personification of the romantic era. It has been said that she was the first to dance on pointe. It is more likely that she was just one of the first, but this new ability to seem to float in the air helped to make her a symbol of poetry and lyricism.

Fanny Elssler and Carlotta Grisi (who created *Giselle*) were two of Taglioni's rivals in the romantic period.

In 1840, the Austrian Elssler came to America. She was not the first European artist to appear in this country (George Amberg notes that foreign dancers have appeared here with regularity since 1789), but her effect was the greatest until that time. She was received so enthusiastically that she stayed for two years. While her tour inspired new interest in ballet in the American public and brought her much personal fame, it took many years and the prima ballerina assoluta, Anna Pavlova, to make ballet an intrinsic part of American culture.

It is wise at this point to pause and examine for a moment how the different styles and techniques of nations and teachers have been passed along to you, the 20th century student. As we mentioned earlier, Carlo Blasis was the originator of the traditional exercises at the barre. Blasis was the teacher of Giovanni Lepri, who in turn taught Enrico Cecchetti. Cecchetti went to Russia, where he became one of the the great 19th century ballet masters, along with Marius Petipa of France. Petipa was also a renowned choreographer. Cecchetti introduced new ideas of his own, but retained most of Blasis' work, which has come down through many years and many nations to remain the basis from which contemporary ballet dancers function.

Grace and purity were the trademarks of the French, strong technique and virtuosity of the Italians. The Russians combined the two schools, leaning somewhat toward the French, while projecting the drama, the strength, and the earthy realism contained in their own peasant folk dancing.

Although ballet had been growing and maturing in Europe for many years, it was the visit to Russia in 1907 of an American dancer that helped bring about changes in the concept of ballet which remain with us today.

The visitor was Isadora Duncan. Duncan was a revolutionary in dance. She rejected the toe shoe and danced barefoot. She wore Grecian tunics instead of tights and tutus. Her music was of the kind that, up to that time, had been heard mainly in concert. Her choreography was an interpretation of the emotions the music stirred in her. She emphasized what she felt was "natural."

Duncan's feelings about dance somewhat influenced Michel Fokine, of the Russian Imperial Ballet. Fokine was also a revolutionary in dance. He wanted to keep what was good in ballet and ballet training, but felt that much of the ballet routine was artificial and overdone.

Fokine mounted two ballets which were much shorter than the usual full-length evening. These ballets featured shoeless dancers—toes were painted on the feet of their tights! The ballets met with such violent criticism that Fokine and his friends might well have given up the attempt to reform ballet along more rational lines had it not been for a young man of vision, a man who felt his mission was to bring the new Russian ballet to the European public.

This man was Serge Diaghilev. Dia-ghilev was neither a dancer nor an artist, but he was acquainted with many forms of art and was vitally interested in them all.

While the inability to obtain a government subsidy and permission to take a ballet company abroad forced Diaghilev at first to present only Russian painting and music to the world outside Russia, he did not lose sight of his dream to produce ballet. Finally, after years of difficulty, he brought dancers from the Maryinsky Theatre Ballet of St. Petersburg to Paris in 1909. The works of Fokine formed the major part of the repertoire, and among the dancers were Pavlova, Karsavina, Nijinsky, Fokine himself, Bolm and Mordkin.

With such dancers, such a choreographer, and exciting new costume and set designers like Leon Bakst and Alexandre Benois, it is not surprising that the Maryinsky company met with fabulous success. Success is too mild a term: Paris was in an uproar. So, later, was London, then all of western Europe, and finally the United States.

Among artists whose careers were helped by Diaghilev were Fokine, Leonide Massine, George Balanchine, Vaslav Nijinsky; composers included Igor Stravinsky and Maurice Ravel; and among the designers were Picasso, Chagall, Bakst and Cocteau.

In 1910, Anna Pavlova came to America. It was a momentous event, for Pavlova's arrival marked the coming of age of ballet in America. We had had European dancers visit us, and several fine dancers of our own had developed. But nothing like Pavlova had ever happened to us before.

She was magic. Perhaps it was in part due to the legend that preceded her, perhaps to the greatness of the ballerina herself. The exact cause does not really matter: she came—with Michael Mordkin as partner—and America has never been quite the same.

At the end of their second tour, Pavlova and Mordkin separated. He stayed in New York to teach, while Pavlova toured the States frequently until 1925. Mordkin, among others, was building new dancers, and Pavlova was creating an audience for them.

Little girls who saw the great ballerina at matinees—among them Agnes de Mille—began to beg for lessons, and their parents, sometimes reluctantly, agreed. Other companies from Europe followed Pavlova and heightened American interest in this wonderful "new" art. In the Twenties and Thirties dancers and choreographers started to come here from Europe to perform, teach, and help build new companies. One of these artists was George Balanchine.

And with the emergence of our own companies there came a new style. We now have three national companies with three distinct styles. These are discussed in Chapter Four. Each of them has something particularly American.

Our companies are not state-subsidized like the European companies, and exist only because there are enthusiastic supporters of American ballet who contribute to maintain them. Many people argue in favor of government subsidy for our companies but, whether this would be better or not, it is wonderfully encouraging that our companies continue to produce fine ballets on low budgets and have become as well known and praised abroad as they are in their own country.

The magical ballerina, Anna Pavlova. She bewitched America and enchanted the world

Melissa Hayden and Jacques D'Amboise—principal dancers in Figure in the Carpet

Chapter Six

BALLERINA

*Your life as a featured dancer, the
'greats' and the promising
dancers of American ballet today*

When you saw that first ballet so long ago, all you could think about was the glorious lady in the spotlight, the prima ballerina, the star. Now several years have gone by.

The chances are that, as you've been steadily working and gaining ground in your profession, your goal has been focused not only on stardom with its magic solitary spotlight, but on the next rung up the company ladder. With increased labor and a real push to learn as many roles in the repertoire as you can, you discover that you've climbed another rung: you are being used in smaller and smaller groups and, frequently, you have a tiny bit all your own.

This should only make you work harder. For now you have a new inner knowledge—your efforts have been seen and are being rewarded. You are being watched, and developed, and groomed. By now your technique should be so strong and sure that you can pay more attention to the things that will make the difference between your remaining a very good dancer or becoming an artist.

You turn again to interpretation. If you were the captured Firebird, would you be frightened and timid, pleading and entreating, or would you let anger and outrage show at such treatment? Would you beg or would you demand to be freed? You will read about the great performances of *Giselle* and of how a superb ballerina like Alicia Markova successfully makes the transition between the love-struck young girl and the ethereal Wili. Have you read about Billy the Kid? Do you have your own ideas

77

about what caused his unpredictable rages? You should, if you ever want to dance the part. Every dancer needs a point of view about a character. It may not agree with everyone else's, but it will sustain you and help make your performance real.

In the corps de ballet and as a minor soloist, your main concern has been with the ensemble movement. You have had to raise your arms to the exact height of the dancers' arms on either side of you. The group form and line have been what counted. Individual interpretation would have been out of place. You were there to give background and support to the principals, and to lend atmosphere, feeling, and mood to the ballet. But if your ambition has always been to stand in that spotlight, then you can't afford to have neglected the emotional side of dancing a role, in the classroom and by yourself at home.

Let's go backstage again and see what is going to happen to you next.

There is a group of dancers gathered around the call board in the hall. As they see you coming, they begin to talk excitedly and one of them grabs you by the arm, pointing to a rehearsal schedule tacked to the board. There is to be a special rehearsal of a familiar ballet at 2:30 because a new soloist is going to dance one of the featured roles. And there it is: your name.

You go dizzy for a minute and then start to realize your wonderful luck. One of the soloists is unable to appear and *you* have been chosen to substitute!

It's a marvelous part! You will dance a drum majorette in *Stars and Stripes* and lead the corps de ballet for a quarter of the whole ballet! It is flashy and fun —the kind of part in which you can't help but be noticed!

But—sobering thought—if you're going to be noticed, you had better be good. You might even be reviewed in the newspapers! You have already been taught the part you will dance, but there is a vast difference between rehearsal hall and stage. You rush off to change to practice clothes, trying frantically to go over everything you know about the drum majorette's role.

The rehearsal goes smoothly. You work with the ballet mistress and the male soloist who is to be your partner. You've already danced in the corps of this ballet many times, so you know where it will be in relation to you and feel fairly easy about your exits and entrances. All that watching and studying was not for nothing.

The rest of the day flies by in the flurry of your normal activity. A snack, a short rest, make-up, class. Tonight your dressing table is filled with the good luck tokens of your dressing roommates. There are also notes from your partner and from the ballet mistress.

Back you are at your old post in the wings. There goes the drum roll, there's the count, there are the trumpets, and on you go!

Afterwards you'll probably never remember how you got through it. But you will remember the applause—the lovely,

lovely applause rolling up at you—and the bouquet of roses handed to you during your bow. And the knowledge that, even if you couldn't see them very well through the lights, there were hundreds of people out in the audience who paid good money to see good ballet and, wonder of wonders, they liked you!

Oh, you're not a prima ballerina yet, by any means. But this is the beginning. Some of those people in the audience will take note of your name. Next time they see your company, they'll look for your name on the program and watch for you in the ballets. You have a new responsibility. You are no longer a member of the corps de ballet but a featured soloist. As you appear in more and larger roles, your name will appear in bolder type on the posters in front of the theatre. Your

name may help to sell more tickets!

Even if you make steady progress, adding more and more solos to your credits, your life with the company won't change much. The very top dancers sometimes work as many as fourteen hours a day. But that spotlight you've been craving is finally yours and, if you keep on working and striving, you may be able to keep it burning bright.

You know, of course, that with success, the stars cannot let down and relax, either. The audience knows what each principal can do and demands that he do it or ceases to come see him any more. Success will vanish with a flabby muscle, a few wobbly turns, a series of disappointing leaps. Only constant, unflagging work keeps the stars in the position they occupy.

Russia's prima ballerina assoluta, Ulanova

Tallchief, Magallanes—Allegro Brillante

Fonteyn and Helpmann of the Royal Ballet

The magnificent Alicia Markova as Giselle

However, for the dancer who loves nothing more than the glorious feeling of weightless flight, of projecting profound emotion in a dramatic part, of living and working with some of the greatest artists of our own—or any other—time, every moment will be a unique joy.

There are many fine, talented dancers in America today, but only a very few can hope to climb the last rung of the ladder. You will want to know something about the best contemporary American dancers who have made a place for themselves. Here are a few of them:

DIANA ADAMS was born in Staunton, Virginia, and began studying ballet when she was seven. She went to New York at the age of fifteen, first appearing in the

corps de ballet of *Oklahoma!* and *One Touch of Venus*. Antony Tudor, who was then with Ballet Theatre, saw her dance and arranged for her to join his company. She danced with Ballet Theatre until 1950, when she joined the New York City Ballet.

ALICIA ALONSO started her ballet studies in her native Havana, Cuba. When she was just fifteen, she married Fernando Alonso, also a ballet student. The young couple moved to New York where they appeared with the Mordkin Ballet. In 1939, they joined Ballet Theatre, returning to Cuba each summer to work with the school and company they founded there. Miss Alonso has been given the title, Dama, the highest honor a Cuban woman can receive.

JACQUES D'AMBOISE, premier denseur of the New York City Ballet, was born in Dedham, Massachusetts. He received his training at the School of American Ballet and became a member of the New York City Ballet company at the age of fifteen. He has made many television appearances, was soloist with the Metropolitan Opera Ballet, and has been featured in several motion pictures.

TOD BOLENDER, who comes from Canton, Ohio, came to New York after graduating from high school to study with Hanya Holm. He made his debut in the musical, *Fredericka*. He later enrolled in the School of American Ballet and went with the American Ballet Caravan on its tour of South America in 1941.

Mr. Bolender has developed as choreographer as well as dancer. He has staged the dances for several musical comedies, and the New York City Ballet has his *Souvenirs*, *The Still Point*, and *Creation of the World* in its repertoire.

ANDRE EGLEVSKY was born in Moscow during the first year of the Russian Revolution. His family moved to Paris where he began his study of ballet. Mr. Eglevsky first appeared with the Ballet Russe de Monte Carlo at the age of fourteen. He has been a danseur noble with all the major ballet companies. In 1939, he became a citizen of the United States, and has often appeared with the New York City Ballet since 1951.

Mr. Eglevsky is married to Leda Anchutina, a former ballerina. The Eglevskys run their own ballet school in Massapequa, New York.

ROYES FERNANDEZ was born in New Orleans and is of French-Spanish descent. He studied ballet with Lelia Haller in New Orleans and with Vincenzo Celli in New York. Mr. Fernandez made his professional debut with de Basil's Original Ballet Russe.

He has appeared as principal dancer with Ballet Alicia Alonso, Australia's Borovonsky Ballet, and the San Francisco Ballet. Mr. Fernandez is currently a principal dancer with the American Ballet Theatre.

MELISSA HAYDEN was born in Toronto, Canada, and began her ballet training there with the Volkoff Ballet. She went to New York to continue studying when in her teens and got a job dancing with the ballet at Radio City Music Hall. In 1946 she joined Ballet Theatre as soloist. She remained there until 1949, when she joined the New York City Ballet and became one of its original soloists.

Miss Hayden has opened a school of her own in Cedarhurst, New York.

NORA KAYE, who is from New York City, started her ballet studies with the Metropolitan Opera Ballet School at eight. She was soon having private lessons with Michel Fokine. At fifteen, she enrolled at the School of American Ballet. She appeared with the American Ballet Company at the Metropolitan and joined American Ballet Theatre in 1939. She has been in several musicals and danced as a guest artist with the New York City Ballet.

ALLEGRA KENT, a native of Los Angeles, began her dance training with Bronislava Nijinska and Carmelita Maracci. At fourteen, she went to New York

Perfecting technique is the first—and the most important—part of a dancer's job. Then acting comes into play. Above, Nora Kaye: Fall River Legend, Jardin aux Lilas

Great premier danseur, Igor Youskevitch

where she received a full scholarship to the School of American Ballet. She served as an apprentice at the New York City Ballet and, at fifteen, became a member of that company. Before she was twenty, Miss Kent had become a principal dancer.

JOHN KRIZA was the first native-born American to become principal dancer of a major ballet company. He was born in Berwyn, Illinois. He joined the corps de ballet of American Ballet Theatre in 1940 and worked his way up through the ranks until he became the company's leading male dancer in 1955.

NINA NOVAK, prima ballerina and ballet mistress of Ballet Russe de Monte Carlo,

Allegra Kent and Francisco Moncion, dancers in Moncion's own ballet, **Pastorale**

Young stars of the ballet—Edward Villella and Patricia McBride in The Nutcracker

began her studies when she was eight at the Warsaw Opera Ballet School in Poland. On her second trip to the United States, in 1948, she was seen by Sergei J. Denham, director of Ballet Russe, who invited her to join his company. She has remained there ever since, rising rapidly from the corps de ballet to the rank of prima ballerina.

JEROME ROBBINS is best known for his spectacular choreography. Born in New York City, he began his career as a dancer by studying with his sister Sonya. He then studied with Antony Tudor, Eugene Loring, Ella Daganova and Helene Platova. In 1940, he joined the corps de ballet of Ballet Theatre,

and became a soloist the following year. For that company Mr. Robbins choreographed *Fancy Free, Interplay, Facsimile,* and *Summer Day.*

In 1949, Mr. Robbins joined the New York City Ballet as Associate Artistic Director, a position he still holds.

Among the many musicals Jerome Robbins has choreographed are *Call Me Madam, The King and I, Pajama Game* and *West Side Story.* His own company, Ballets: U.S.A., has recently toured Europe to great acclaim.

LUPE SERRANO was born in Santiago, Chile. She began taking dancing lessons at the age of four. She made her professional debut at the age of thirteen. In

Diana Adams as The Nutcracker's *Sugar Plum Fairy, partnered by André Eglevsky*

Lupe Serrano and Erik Bruhn in American Ballet Theatre's production, Don Quixote

Arthur Mitchell as Puck in New York City Ballet's festive A Midsummer Night's Dream

1951, Miss Serrano went to New York to study with Vincenzo Celli. She appeared with Ballet Russe de Monte Carlo, returned to Mexico for a while, and then joined American Ballet Theatre in 1953. She has risen to principal ballerina rank in that company.

MARIA TALLCHIEF is internationally known as America's leading ballerina. She was born in Fairfax, Oklahoma, and started her dance studies there. When she was eight, her parents moved to Los Angeles and, at twelve, she became a pupil of Bronislava Nijinska. Her first public appearance took place in Hollywood Bowl when she was fifteen. Two years later, in 1942, she made her debut as a member of the corps de ballet of the Ballet Russe de Monte Carlo. In 1947 she joined Ballet Society—which became the New York City Ballet—and was its prima ballerina until 1959. Since then, she has appeared as guest star with the major companies here and in Europe.

VIOLETTE VERDY was born in Brittany and went to Paris to study dance when she was eight. At twelve, she was signed by Les Ballets des Champs-Élysées. Miss Verdy first came to the United States in 1954 with Roland Petit's Ballets de Paris. After an engagement with Ballet Theatre, she joined the New York City Ballet in 1958. Violette Verdy is the first European ballerina to join the company.

EDWARD VILLELLA started studying ballet at the School of American Ballet when he was ten. He joined the New York City Ballet in 1957 and achieved the rank of soloist after only one year. Villella's extraordinary leaps and beats have earned him the praise of such exacting critics as the dancers of the Leningrad Kirov Ballet.

PATRICIA WILDE is from Canada and began taking lessons in her native Ottawa. She went to New York to study with Dorothie Littlefield and the School of American Ballet. Miss Wilde later joined the Marquis de Cuevas' Ballet International and, in 1945, became a soloist with the Ballet Russe de Monte Carlo. With Ballet Russe, she toured Europe and the United States and joined the New York City Ballet in 1950.

IGOR YOUSKEVITCH—born in Russia and brought up in Yugoslavia—was a student of chemical engineering when he was persuaded to make ballet his career in 1932. He made his debut after only one year of lessons. He joined the Ballet Russe de Monte Carlo in 1938 and made his first appearance with that company in this country. In 1943 he went into the United States Navy. Two years later he danced with Ballet Theatre, and then rejoined Ballet Russe in 1955. He has frequently toured with Alicia Alonso and is her favorite partner.

GEORGE ZORITCH was born in Moscow and raised in Kovno, Lithuania. He started taking ballet lessons at eleven, and studied with Leonide Massine and Olga Preobrajenska. He was with the Ballet Russe de Monte Carlo when it came to the United States in 1938 and has performed with that company many seasons since then. He is presently the

The dancers bow. The ballet is over. Now you will go back to the classroom—to the barre

premier danseur of Ballet Russe.

All these dancers belong to that special ballet élite, the world of the principal dancer—the star. Ballets are composed to display their particular talents. When a company goes on tour, they—as principals—are especially fêted by their grateful audiences. They are members of a small, glamorous, highly select group—to which, in time and with sincere effort, you may aspire if you have the requisite talent.

There are many young dancers who are working to achieve star status and who are rapidly growing in ability and importance. Here are the names of some of these rising young artists, and you will want to watch their progress.

A dancer from Birmingham, Alabama, Gage Bush first appeared with the Joffrey Theatre Ballet. She is now a member of Ballet Theatre's company.

A student of Carmelita Maracci, Bill Carter comes from Oklahoma but his family moved to Texas when he was little. He became a member of American Ballet Theatre in 1957 and joined the New York City Ballet in 1959. Only two years later, he was promoted to soloist rank. Bill is also interested in choreography and recently appeared in concert in his first two works, *Bach Suite* and *Allegory*.

Gloria Govrin, Newark-born dancer, began studying at the School of American Ballet when she was twelve, though she had been dancing since she was three. In 1958, Miss Govrin was apprenticed to the New York City Ballet and the following year became a regular member of the corps. She is seen increasingly in individual roles.

Bruce Marks, now with the American Ballet Theatre as soloist, was born in

and the mirror—and work until you earn a place on stage in the magical world of ballet

Brooklyn. He attended the High School of Performing Arts and Juilliard School of Music, and received his ballet training at the Metropolitan Opera Ballet School. He has appeared with the Pearl Lang Dance Company and, for two years, was the principal male dancer at the Metropolitan Opera House.

Patricia McBride is from Teaneck, New Jersey, and she started dance study when she was seven. At thirteen, she began classes with Sonya Dobrovinska and at the School of American Ballet. Miss McBride made her professional debut at fifteen with André Eglevsky's Petit Ballet Company. Starting with the New York City Ballet as an apprentice, she became a member of the corps in 1959, was given soloist's billing in 1960, and was the company's youngest principal dancer a year later.

Arthur Mitchell is a native New Yorker and a graduate of the High School of Performing Arts. He received most of his ballet training at the School of American Ballet, and joined the New York City Ballet during its 1954-55 season. Mitchell has been soloist with that company since 1960, and in 1962 was also soloist with the Metropolitan Opera Ballet.

These gifted dancers, and others like them, may be the great ballet stars of tomorrow. Watch them grow, for out of today's young dancers must come tomorrow's great artists.

In a few years, there may be another child sitting in an audience, watching *Swan Lake* for the very first time. She may be gasping in wonder and admiration at the superb dancing of a new Swan Queen.

And who can tell? Perhaps, by method, by a sense of mission, and by a special sort of magic, that great new star could be you!

LANGUAGE OF BALLET

One of the delights of being a dancer is that, wherever you go, you will have a ready-made family waiting for you: the family of dance. Dancers are always eager to meet and talk with other dancers—as *dancers*, not as strangers.

No matter what language other performers speak or what country they come from, you can always communicate. For all ballet positions and steps, many of the gestures, and the status ranks of the ballet companies are the same the world over. They are called, in all countries, by the same names.

To become a part of this world-wide ballet family, you must not only master the positions and steps but the terms most often used in the common language of ballet. Here are some that you will hear over and over again:

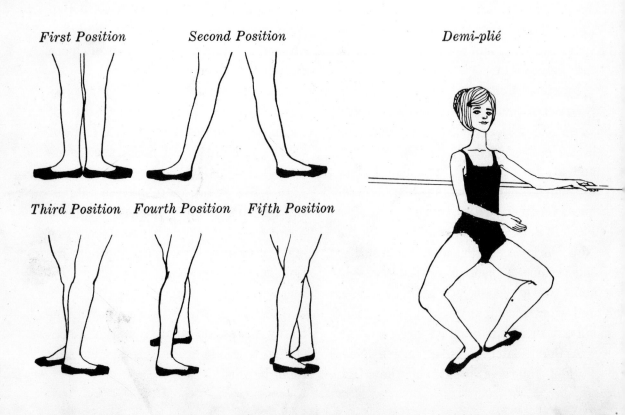

First Position   *Second Position*   *Demi-plié*

Third Position   *Fourth Position*   *Fifth Position*

ADAGIO—A series of exercises executed in the center of the classroom, or any dance executed in slow tempo. As an exercise, adagio develops line, balance, and control, and these are qualities displayed in the adagio dancer. The term also refers to the first (usually slow) part of the classical *pas de deux*, or duet.

ARABESQUE—A position in which the dancer stands with one leg extended in a straight line toward the back. The supporting leg may be bent or straight. There are many kinds of arabesques, depending on whether the body is held erect or tilted forward, and also on the various positions of the head and arms.

ATTITUDE—Like the arabesque, but the raised leg is bent, sometimes only slightly but usually (in America) to a 90° angle.

BALANCÉ—A rocking step from one foot to the other, usually done in waltz time.

BALLERINA—Literally a "dancer," but now used to designate a leading female dancer, a star. A prima ballerina is the outstanding female dancer in a company or even in a country.

BARRE—The wooden bar or railing usually placed about waist-high that the dancer uses for support when doing exercises. Also the se-

ries of exercises practiced there.

BATTEMENT—Literally, "beating." This refers to a number of movements in which the leg beats into the air, i.e. moves away from the supporting leg and body. In a *battement tendu* —a stretched beat—the leg slides out along the floor until the foot is completely pointed but still touches the floor. In a *battement dégagé*— a freed beat—the foot rises just clear of the floor. In a *grand battement*—a great beat—the leg is raised high in the air. Battements are done as exercises to develop strength and control. They are also used as parts of steps.

BATTERIE—A succession of beats. The term is used to refer to jumps during which the dancer beats his legs together, opening and closing them while in the air. *Cabrioles* and *entrechats* (see below) are forms of batterie.

CABRIOLE—A jump in which the dancer makes a grand battement with one leg, raises the supporting leg to beat under the free leg, and lands once more on the supporting leg.

CHANGEMENT—A jump from the fifth position in which the front leg passes to the back while the dancer is in the air. He lands in the fifth position with the opposite foot in front.

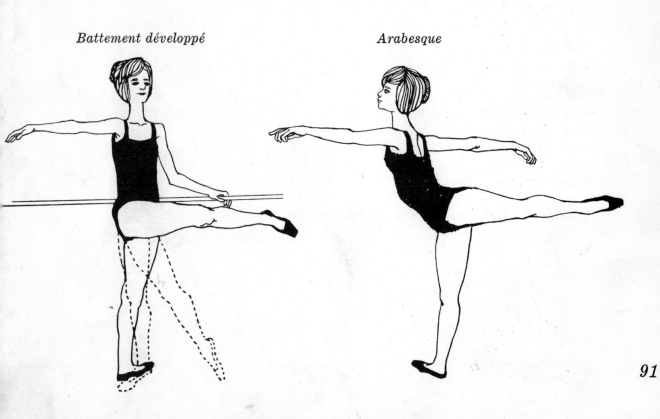

Battement développé   *Arabesque*

CORPS DE BALLET—The ensemble or group dancers of a ballet company.

DÉVELOPPÉ—The gradual extension of the leg as it is lifted from the floor. This may be performed to the front, side or back, and the impression is of an unfolding or "development" of the raised leg. The supporting leg is bent at the beginning of the movement but it is in straight position when the full extension, or stretch, of the lifted leg is reached.

DIVERTISSEMENT—A suite of dances designed to show the technical skills of the dancers. It has little or no relation to the story line of the ballet.

ELEVATION—Referring to the dancer: his ability to jump. Referring to the dance: a dance involving many jumps or much movement in the air, as contrasted with *terre à terre* dancing which is close to the ground.

ENTRECHAT—A jump during which the legs beat, changing their front-back relationship. Entrechats are described according to the number of times the legs change their position in the air. Thus, if the dancer changes the position of his legs four times, it is called an *entrechat quatre*.

ÉPAULEMENT—Literally, "shouldering." The dancer turns the body from the waist upward, so that one shoulder appears forward of the body line. Epaulement is used to give variety and nuance, or shading, to the standard ballet positions.

FIVE POSITIONS—These are the basic positions of the feet in the classic ballet. (Study them in the illustrations.)

FOUETTÉ—A *fouet* means literally a whip, and the movement is a turn in which the working leg is whipped around the supporting leg. This gives impetus or drive to the turn. Fouettés are usually done in series and very fast.

GLISSADE—This is a sliding movement in which the dancer starts from the fifth position, separates his legs, and then returns them to the fifth position.

JETÉ—Literally, "thrown." One leg is raised (thrown) into the air while the dancer springs off the supporting foot, rises into the air, and lands on the foot that was thrown. A jeté may be small, but the best known one is the *grand jeté*, a leap that travels high and wide.

PAS—A step or dance. When used with a French numeral, this describes the number of

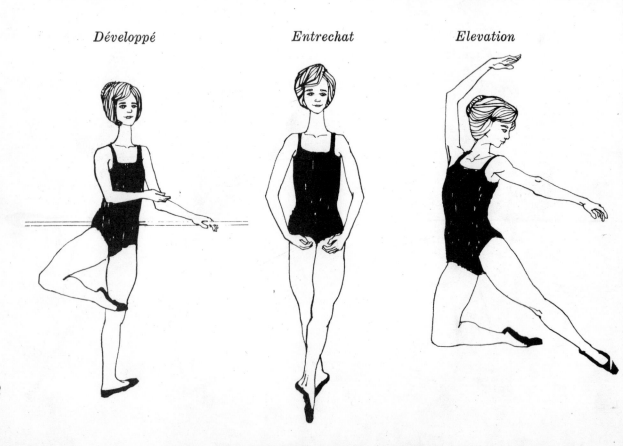

Développé   *Entrechat*   *Elevation*

persons taking part in a dance. Thus *pas de deux*, dance for two, or duet; *pas de trois*, dance for three; *pas de dix*, dance for ten.

PAS D'ACTION—These are passages in a dance that combine steps with pantomime and that advance the plot of a story ballet, or explain how the dance characters feel about each other.

PAS DE POISSON—This is the great sweeping movement that usually occurs at the end of a sequence of steps when the ballerina seems to fly toward the opposite side of the stage in a great fishlike arching. Her swoop is caught in the arms of her partner as her body bends upward from the floor which she seems nearly to have touched.

PIROUETTE—Any complete turn executed on one foot.

PLIÉ—Literally, "bent." The knees bend while the hips, legs and feet are turned out. A *demi-plié* is a half or small bend.

POINTE—This refers to the tips of the ballerina's toe shoes. Dancing on pointe, or *sur les pointes*, means rising and moving on the tips of the toes. The ballerina wears hard or blocked toes which supports her raised-foot position.

PORT DE BRAS—Literally, carriage of the arms. There are basic arm positions in classic ballet, just as there are the five traditional foot positions.

RELEVÉ—A rise from a demi-plié to a position on pointe or demi-pointe.

SPOTTING—The practice, in performing pirouettes, of focussing the eyes on one spot and snapping the head around more quickly than the body in order to keep the focus. The dancer does this to prevent dizziness.

TOUR EN L'AIR—A complete turn in the air. The double and even triple turn is reserved for male dancers. The movement starts from the fifth position and from a demi-plié, with the dancer leaping straight up, executing a complete turn, and returning to the position from which he started.

TURNOUT—This is the traditional position of the ballet dancer, whose feet and legs are turned outward at the hips.

TUTU—The ballerina's traditional skirt. The romantic tutu reaches to a line a little above the ankle, while in classic ballet it is cut short so that the net-layered skirt reveals the full length of the dancer's legs.

Grand-jeté   Tour en l'air   Glissade (echappé)

BOOKS
ABOUT BALLET

by SELMA JEANNE COHEN

GENERAL HISTORIES

Guest, Ivor. THE DANCER'S HERITAGE. New York, Macmillan, 1961. 156p. illus. Written as a basic text in ballet history at the Royal Ballet School. An excellent introduction.

Haskell, Arnold. BALLET; a complete guide to appreciation: history, aesthetics, ballets, dancers. Rev. ed. Harmondsworth, Middlesex, Penguin Books, 1951. 211p. illus. Paper bound, containing a guide to the art of ballet, a glossary of terms, decorations by Kay Ambrose.

Haskell, Arnold. A PICTURE HISTORY OF THE BALLET. London, Hulton Press, 1954. 24p. plus 588 illus. A fascinating chronicle of the ballet. The illustrations are generally well chosen, and the volume as a whole is a pleasant companion to printed histories of the dance.

Kinney, Troy, and Margaret West. THE DANCE, its place in art and life. New York, Stokes, 1924. 334p. illus. A general survey beginning with Egypt, with unusually broad coverage of folk dances of Europe, the Near East, and the Orient. Excellent photographs.

Kirstein, Lincoln. DANCE; A short history of classic theatrical dancing. New York, G. P. Putnam, 1935. 369p. illus. The most complete contemporary survey in English. The best chapters are those dealing with ballet.

Lynham, Deryck. BALLET THEN AND NOW; a history of the ballet in Europe. London, Sylvan Press, 1947. 214p. illus. A fine introduction. The author has consulted orig-

inal sources, as well as published studies.

Martin, John. THE DANCE; the story of the dance told in pictures and text. New York, Tudor, 1946. 160p. illus. Devoted principally to "the dance as spectacle," with particular attention to ballet and modern dance.

Moore, Lillian. "BALLET," Encyclopedia Britannica, 1959. 11p. illus. Concisely, but with plenty of vivid detail, the author traces the evolution of ballet technique and productions. Accurate, clear and excitingly written. Contains a section on technique.

SURVEYS OF OUR TIME

Martin, John. WORLD BOOK OF MODERN BALLET. Cleveland, World Pub. Co., 1952. 191p. illus. (part color). A history of ballet since the death of Diaghilev, told in a lovely, cogent manner. Principal emphasis is on the dance in America, with briefer treatment of French and British developments.

UNITED STATES

Amberg, George. BALLET IN AMERICA; the emergence of an American art. New York, Duell, Sloan and Pearce, 1949. xx, 244p. illus. The author sketches the early history of ballet in America, but his principal interests lie in the modern developments of choreography, the rise of American dancers, and the emergence of the ballet as a part of American life.

Magriel, Paul, ed. CHRONICLES OF THE AMERICAN DANCE. New York, Holt, 1948. xii, 268p. illus. A collection of essays from *Dance Index* that tell—in tantalizing fragments—the high points of dance history in the United States. The Shakers, early minstrelsey, ballroom dancing, the ballet, and the modern

This list of books is taken from a fuller bibliography Miss Cohen prepared for *Dance Magazine* (March-August, 1961) and is reprinted with the kind permission of that magazine.

dance. These articles should make every American dancer proud of his heritage.

Terry, Walter. THE DANCE IN AMERICA. New York, Harper, 1956. 248p. illus. A readable account of developments since 1900. Considers the field broadly, including ballet, modern dance, musical comedies, films, education.

COMPANY HISTORIES
AMERICAN BALLET THEATRE

Cohen, Selma Jeanne, and A. J. Pischl. "THE AMERICAN BALLET THEATRE: 1940-1960," Dance Perspectives 6 (spring, 1960). 124p. illus. A chronology of all ballets produced by the company, with excerpts from reviews. The nature of repertory provides a picture of contemporary taste and creative activity.

BOLSHOI BALLET

THE BOLSHOI BALLET STORY. New York, Heller & Heller, 1959. 128p. illus. Essays by Y. Bocharnikova and M. Gabovich on the Bolshoi School, by Galina Ulanova on "the making of a ballerina," and by Yuri Slonimsky on the history of the company.

NEW YORK CITY BALLET

Chujoy, Anatole. THE NEW YORK CITY BALLET. New York, Knopf, 1953. xiii, 382, xv p. illus. A carefully documented study of one of America's finest companies, from its inception with the establishment of the School of American Ballet in 1934 through the European tour of the troupe in 1952.

ROYAL BALLET (SADLER'S WELLS)

Clarke, Mary. THE SADLER'S WELLS BALLET; a history and an interpretation. London, A. & C. Black, 1955. xv-336p. illus. A serious, carefully documented history, informal in style, it nevertheless provides a fine basis for appreciation of Britain's national ballet.

REFERENCE BOOKS

Chujoy, Anatole, ed. THE DANCE ENCYCLOPEDIA. New York, Barnes, 1949. xvi, 546p. Basic for general reference. Emphasizes Western theatrical dance. Contains biographical sketches, short definitions and explanations, as well as longer articles by such writers as Edwin Denby, Walter Terry and George Amberg. Includes a bibliography of books in English, and a discography of dance music.

DICTIONARY OF MODERN BALLET. Francis Gadan and Robert Maillard, eds. Selma Jeanne Cohen, American ed. New York, Tudor, 1959. 360p. illus. (part color). Originally produced in France, and emphasizing French ballet, this book also appears in British and German editions. Its articles are very uneven in quality, but the illustrations, especially the color reproductions of decor and costume designs, provide a beautiful pictorial survey of 20th-century ballet.

Wilson, George B. L. A DICTIONARY OF BALLET. Harmondsworth, Penguin Books, 1957. 283p. A small paperback with a large amount of information. The entries are brief but accurate, covering technical terms, ballets, dancers, companies and choreographers from the 16th century to the present.

APPRECIATION

Fisher, Hugh. THE BALLET. New York, Crowell, 1953. 95p. illus. An introduction to the ballet for young people, with chapters devoted to the roles played by the choreographer, the composer, the designer, and the dancer. The language avoids technicalities, but presupposes intelligence on the part of the young reader. Suitable for adults as well.

Franks, Arthur H. GIRL'S BOOK OF BALLET. London, Burke, 1953. 144p. illus. (part color). Essays by such notables as Beryl Grey, Gene Kelly, and Arnold Haskell, with commentary on the photographs by P. W. Manchester and Lillian Moore. Two original dances, with choreography and music suitable for the young dancer, are provided.

BALLET STORIES:
COLLECTIONS

Balanchine, George. COMPLETE STORIES OF THE GREAT BALLETS. Edited by Francis Mason. Annotated selection of recordings by Jacques Fray. Drawings by Marta Becket. Garden City, N.Y., Doubleday, 1954. xviii, 615p. illus. Much more than a plot book, this excellent work includes historical notes, a brief history of ballet, and a discussion of practical aspects of the dance—ballet for children, careers in ballets, etc. A mine of information, especially about the actual choreography of many ballets in the current repertory.

Index